REVISE FOR RELIGIOUS STUDIES GCSE

for Edexcel

Religion and Life

Sarah K. Tyler
and
Gordon Reid

heinemann.co.uk
✓ Free online support
✓ Useful weblinks
✓ 24 hour online ordering

01865 888058

Inspiring generations

Heinemann is an imprint of Pearson Education Limited, a company incorporated in
England and Wales, having its registered office at Edinburgh Gate, Harlow, Essex, CM20 2JE.
Registered company number: 872828

Heinemann is the registered trademark of
Pearson Education Limited

© Sarah K. Tyler and Gordon Reid, 2004

First published 2004

09
10 9 8 7 6 5 4

British Library Cataloguing in Publication Data is available
from the British Library on request.

ISBN 978 0 435307 10 3

Designed and typeset by TechType, Abingdon, Oxon

Original illustrations © Harcourt Education Limited, 2004

Illustrated by TechType, Abingdon, Oxon
Printed in the UK by Scotprint
Cover photo: © Alamy
Picture research by Kath Kollberg

Acknowledgements
The New International Version of the Bible has been used for all biblical references and The Wordsworth Classics
of World Literature edition of the Qur'an has been used for all Qur'an references.

The publishers would like to thank the following for permission to reproduce photographs: p.9 Rex Features; p.12
Science and Society Picture Library; p.16 Alamy; p.23 Bridgeman Art Library; p.29 Mark Cambell/Photofusion;
p.38 AP Photo/Charles Rex Arbogast; p.41 Hulton Getty; p.49 Mary Evans Picture Library; p.51 E&E/WP Edwards;
p.52 Panos; p.56 Corbis; p.63 BBC; p.69 Kobal Collection; p.82 Panos; p.83 Still Pictures/Christian Aid/Jacinta Fox;
p.85 Muslim Aid.

Every effort has been made to contact copyright holders of material reproduced in this book. Any omissions will
be rectified in subsequent printings if notice is given to the publisher.

Websites
There are links to relevant websites in this book. In order to ensure that the links are up-to-date, that the links
work, and that the sites are not inadvertently linked to sites that could be considered offensive, we have made the
links available on the Heinemann website at www.heinemann.co.uk/hotlinks. When you access the website, enter
the express code **710XP**, and this will take you to the links you want.

Tel: 01865 888058 www.heinemann.co.uk

Contents

Religion and life has been designed to give you access to the information you need to gain top grades in the Edexcel Religious Studies GCSE course, which follows the Religion and Life specification. It deals with all six specification areas, looking at Unit A: Religion and life from the perspective of Christianity and one other religion – in this case, Islam. You will also find the material relevant and useful for Units B (Christianity) and Unit C (Catholic Christianity). The six specification areas are:

- Believing in God
- Matters of life and death
- Marriage and the family
- Social harmony
- Religion and the media (can be examined or covered by coursework)
- Religion: wealth and poverty (can be examined or covered by coursework).

These correspond exactly with what you will find in the specification, and at the beginning of each chapter there is a list of what you need to know. At the end of each chapter there is a checklist for revision, reminding you of these areas, so you can continually keep track of how your learning is progressing.

The exam paper

In the exam you will have to answer either four or five questions, depending on whether you are offering coursework. If you are doing coursework, each exam question you answer is broken down into four parts. The total mark available is 20 and the marks for each part break down in to (a) 2 marks, (b) 6 marks, (c) 8 marks and (d) 4 marks. The 2-mark question usually asks for a definition of a key term or idea. The 6-mark question asks you to show your knowledge of a belief or issue. The 8-mark question aims to

see how well you understand the issues and beliefs. Finally, the 4-mark question asks you to consider a point of view and weigh up arguments for and against it, giving your own opinion in a carefully considered way.

If you are not doing coursework, but answering a fifth question in the exam, you will have to write longer answers for this part. The question is broken down into three parts, (a) worth 4, (b) worth 8 and (c) worth 8 marks. The 4-mark question is still knowledge based, asking you for information and facts about the topic. The first 8-mark question asks you to show your understanding of the topic. The second 8-mark question is evaluative – again suggesting a point of view and asking you to analyse it and make a balanced judgement.

You will need to work quickly in the exam as there is a lot to cover. Additionally, you need to remember that if you offer the fifth specification area in the exam, you are being tested for quality of writing as well as content.

If you offer coursework, then you will still be answering a very similar set of questions to those you will find in the exam, but you will inevitably write more and go into more depth. The specification suggests 1500 words for a piece of coursework, although you can write more than that. The coursework questions are broken down into two parts, again worth 20 marks in total. Part **a** consists of three sub-questions, which are knowledge and understanding based and worth 12 marks. Part **b** consists of one 8-mark evaluation question, as in the exam. You are likely to get plenty of guidance from your teacher about coursework, but the key is not to rush it at the last minute – take time to perfect it, try to get in some information that no one else in your class has in theirs and present it so that it is a pleasure for the examiner to read. There is a lot of coursework out there and you need to make sure yours is of a high standard.

This book will serve several functions.

- It will give you information that you might not already have.
- It will help you to revise material you do already have access to.
- It will show you the best way to tackle things in the exam.

Quotations

You will see that each chapter includes several quotations from religious texts and other sources, and you should aim to learn a few of these for each specification area. Every topic covers a range of views and this is very important, as you cannot get top marks if you do not show that you are aware of and can discuss the differences in belief on even some of the most central issues in religion.

How this book is organized

Each chapter begins with 'What do I need to know?', which outlines information you will need to answer examination questions on the topic.

Margin features

Did you know?
Short pieces of information that are useful additions to your knowledge and can be used as examples in examination answers.

Hints and tips
Brief guidelines designed to assist revision and examination technique.

Exam watch
Brief tips to help you achieve better marks in your exam.

Key ideas
Short points that summarize the main points in a section.

key ideas

Beware
Tips to help you avoid commonly made mistakes in the exam.

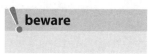

Action point
Brief exercises that you can practise to help you revise.

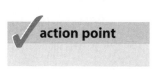

Read more
Suggestions for further reading to help you add more detail to your answers. These may also direct you to another section of the book where passages or topics are explained in more detail.

Key words

Important words and terms appear in bold print the first time they appear in the book. Definitions of these words can be found in the Glossary on pages 91–4. You should learn these and be prepared to explain them. Where glossary terms appear in the Edexcel specification glossary we have used these definitions.

Sample questions

There are sample exam questions and answers at the end of each chapter reflecting the kinds of questions you are likely to get in the exam. For every question an excellent answer is provided that is easily worth the full marks it would be given. In some instances a more sophisticated answer than would be required to gain full marks has been included to help raise the standards of even the most able pupils. These excellent answers are useful because you need to know what is the best you could aim to achieve. For some of the questions there are also answers showing the build up of marks, which clearly demonstrates how to gain marks in the exam.

Do not be afraid to write in this book – use highlighters and colours freely. It really helps your learning, and it will make this book yours rather than just ours.

exam watch

What do I need to know?

- The ways in which people may come to believe in God.

- How special events and situations may encourage people's beliefs.

- How features of the world contribute to a person's religious belief.

- How many of these same features, and others, may contribute to doubt about belief in God.

- The relationship between belief in God and the qualities associated with him.

You should base your answers to questions in this chapter on one religion only.

Coming to believe in God

People who believe in the existence of God – whether they call themselves Christians, Muslims or Jews, or who may not even be formally associated with any one particular faith – are likely to have come to that belief through one or more of a number of possible ways. Everyone has their own story to tell about why they believe in God.

Christians and Muslims believe in one God. This is known as monotheism, which distinguishes these religions from others that acknowledge more than one God. The central belief of Islam is *'La ilaha ilallah wa Muhammadur rasul al-Lah'* (There is no God but Allah, and Muhammad is the Prophet of God). This is known as the Shahada, and it highlights the two essential truths of the faith:

- that there is One God, Supreme and Unique

- that the revelation given through the Prophet Muhammad is the final and complete revelation of God, which is above all that came before it.

Anyone who becomes a Muslim must say and accept the truth of the Shahada.

For Christians, the fact that Jesus is believed to be the Son of God does not mean that there is more than one God. God the Holy Spirit, God the Son and God the Father are all considered to be the one person of God. This could be illustrated as below:

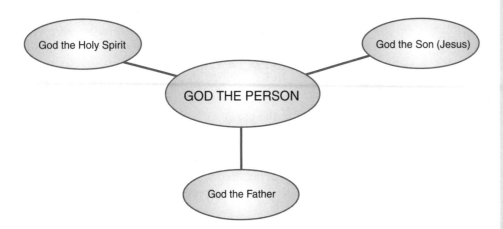

God the Holy Spirit — GOD THE PERSON — God the Son (Jesus) — God the Father

> **beware**
>
> Don't fall into the trap of saying 'All Christians believe …' or 'Everyone who believes in God thinks …', – it would be almost impossible to find something that they all agreed on!

> **key idea**
>
> *'Whatever ye are given here is but a convenience of this life; but that which is with Allah is better and more lasting; it is for those who believe and put their trust in their Lord. Those who avoid the greater crimes and shameful deeds, and where they are angry, even then forgive. Those who hearken to their Lord and establish regular prayer …'* (Surah 42: 36–8)

Family and the community

Traditionally, the family, and both the local and wider community, have played a significant part in the way in which many people come to believe in God and in the way that belief is reflected in their lifestyle and practices. For a good number of religious believers, their faith is probably closely associated with the beliefs that their parents and their **extended family** hold. Their family life is often bound together by that faith. They tend to see it as an important part of their heritage, something that is handed down from one generation to the next, and the truth of which they probably would never question.

Shared belief between family members and members of the community is very important in preserving belief in God and maintaining the importance of religion for generations to come. It can also unite the family and the community, helping them to stand against opposition and giving them a special identity. Families and communities also support their faith through shared practices. These may include:

- praying and worshipping together and with other members of their faith

- witnessing to other communities or individuals (telling them about their faith)

- taking care of each other and encouraging one another in difficult times

- celebrating religious festivals and sacraments

- rejoicing together and thanking God for good things.

Christian families are likely to introduce children to the faith through baptism. Here they will make promises to bring up their children in a Christian environment and to teach them the fundamentals of the faith. Attendance at Sunday School and church, where God's existence is taken for granted, will encourage children to see belief in God as something that is relevant and meaningful.

The first words Muslim children are likely to hear are 'God is great' whispered in their ear after they are born. When they are older they generally attend madrasah, the mosque school, and their family are likely to make observance of Ramadam (the month-long fast) a central part of establishing a Muslim identity for their child.

Growing up as a Muslim, a child will learn that actions must be done for God's sake only, not to gain praise or fame. Actions must be performed in accordance with the Al-Sunnah. These are the rules, orders, acts of worship, and statements. However, although a Muslim can only be held accountable for that which they know, they should take the time to learn about things they do not know, to ask questions and to follow the example of experienced Muslims.

One of the most important things to learn about will be the five pillars of Islam. As well as testifying that none has the right to be worshipped but God and that Muhammad is God's Messenger, the other four pillars are:

- Salah – offering the compulsory congregational prayers dutifully

- **Zakah** – a specific charity paid yearly for the benefit of poor Muslims (2.5% of **wealth**)

- Hajj – pilgrimage to Makka

- to observe fast during the month of Ramadan.

did you know?

There are approximately 1.2 billion Muslims worldwide. About 21% of all people on earth follow Islam. Christianity, meanwhile, is currently the largest religion in the world. It is followed by about 33% of all people.

key idea

Richard Dawkins claims that children should be referred to as 'a child of Muslim parents', for example, not as being Muslim themselves.

did you know?

Christian and Muslim parents may both choose to send their children to religious schools for their general education.

Personal experience

Not everyone comes to believe in God because they belong to a family or community that encourages such belief. In the modern world, many people have been brought up without a traditional religious background. Yet they still find faith in God through personal experience. Some people believe that this leads to a more genuine faith and argue that everyone must find a personal reason to believe in God. Personal experience keeps faith alive. Many people over the centuries have claimed that vivid, personal and direct experience of God has convinced them of his existence in a way that nothing else could. There are three special types of personal experience:

- **religious experience**
- **miracles**
- **prayer**.

Religious experience

There are many varieties of religious experience, all of which may come under the description of an encounter with God. Such an encounter might include **mystical experiences**, for example:

- hearing God's voice
- seeing a vision of a religious figure – perhaps Jesus or a saint
- a dream that offered divine guidance
- a **near-death experience**
- a **charismatic** experience – speaking in tongues, prophecy or healing
- a miracle, or a **conversion** experience, when a person is converted from one faith to another or from having no faith at all to belief in God.

Some conversion experiences can be quite dramatic, such as that of the apostle Paul. Others might be the result of years of quiet searching for God. Whatever forms the experience takes, it is the feelings it generates that are perhaps the most important. A religious experience is often described as being **numinous**. Numinous describes feelings of awe (holy fear and wonder), a heightened spiritual awareness and a sense of being either very close to God or very separated from him. An increased love for God and a desire to serve him are likely to be results of a genuine religious experience.

Miracles

Miracles are a special category of religious experience and are most often described as events that break a natural law. A natural law is something that happens so frequently within the world – for example, the sun rising and setting – that it would be considered miraculous (beyond the workings of nature) if it happened differently or failed to happen when it was expected to do so. For religious believers, God is thought to be the best explanation for why such an unexpected event might take place. If someone is healed of cancer, for example, or a blind person recovers their sight with no explanation, then it may be convincing enough to lead someone to believe in God or to support the faith of someone who already believes.

read more

Read the account of Saul's conversion in Acts 9: 1–19, and of Nicky Cruz, a dangerous gang leader, in his book *Run, Baby, Run*. This is a true story, but if you prefer a novel about conversion, read *The Heartbreaker*, by Susan Howatch.

action point

Visit www. heinemann.co.uk /hotlinks and click on this section to read an account of the singer Cat Stevens' conversion to Islam.

exam watch

You should be able to recount accurately one biblical miracle, and offer two or three clear points about its meaning and significance.

The Christian perspective

Jesus was a miracle worker. In the gospels he is described as curing the sick and paralysed, calming storms, feeding crowds with very little food and even raising the dead. After his death and **resurrection**, the apostles and other members of the early church also performed miracles. It was clearly something that was part of their regular experience.

Today, many religious believers continue to believe that God performs miracles and that we should not be surprised to hear about miraculous events. Some people attend huge rallies led by charismatic leaders such as Benny Hinn or Rheinhard Bonnke, during which hundreds of people claim to have been healed. Others believe that miracles have taken place in their church or quietly as they pray.

Read Mark 4: 35–41 (the calming of the storm); Luke 8: 40–56 (Jairus's daughter and the woman with the haemorrhage); Matthew 14: 13–21 (the feeding of the 5000); John 11: 1–44 (the raising of Lazarus); and Acts 3: 1–10 (the healing of the crippled man).

read more

Benny Hinn

Benny Hinn has established himself as a world-renowned evangelist, teacher and miracle worker, although he is always careful to say that his healing power is God's power working through him, not his alone. Hinn has a daily programme on Trinity Network Broadcasting, called *This is Your Day*, which is broadcast all over the world.

He is also the author of several books, including the best selling *Good Morning Holy Spirit*. He was the pastor of the Orlando Christian Centre in Florida, but moved his base to Dallas in 1999. Thousands of people see Benny Hinn preach and go to his miracle crusades in the hope of being healed from terminal illnesses and severe physical disabilities, and many have claimed to receive that healing. However, Benny Hinn is a very controversial figure and many well-known and respected Christian writers and preachers speak out strongly against him and his claims.

The Islamic perspective

Islam believes that a number of miracles were bestowed on and performed by the Prophet Muhammad, which proved his calling. The greatest of these was the revelation of the Qur'an, which is thought to be perfect and inimitable in its language and style, and appears to have been **verified** in various ways by historical, archaeological and scientific discoveries. Muslims believe that, unlike the miracles of other prophets before Muhammad, the miracle of the Qur'an is **eternal**. Muhammad is also credited with splitting the moon, providing miraculous supplies of food and water, providing lights to guide his companions on a dark night and appealing for rain in a time of drought.

Modern miracles are sometimes claimed within Islam, though they seem quite different to those acclaimed within contemporary Christianity. In 1997, a

Huddersfield teenager sliced open a tomato to find that the veins of the two halves appeared to spell out in Arabic, 'There is only one God' and 'Muhammad is the messenger'. Claims that similar messages have been read in melons, aubergines, honeycomb and eggs periodically appear in the news. According to another account, a young man in the Netherlands purchased 5 kilos of beans and found the word 'God' inscribed on several of them. When he donated the beans to the mosque to form the basis of a meal for the community, the imam later reported, 'We could serve as much as we wished, and the supply was still not exhausted.'

Some other perspectives

Many religious believers will claim that if God exists, then we should not be surprised that he performs miracles. If he is **all-loving** and **all-powerful** – two of the most important qualities associated with God – then we should expect him to meet the needs of those who believe in him by intervening miraculously in their lives. If he did so during biblical times, then there is no reason not to expect him to continue to do so today, since God is unchanging and eternal.

key idea

There are many attributes and characteristics of God that believers consider to be a very important part of understanding him. Unchanging and eternal are two of them. Make sure you are familiar with the meaning of these words.

Prayer

Prayer is perhaps the most common way in which religious believers communicate with God. It may involve words or be silent, but in either case, prayer assumes that God has a relationship with those who pray to him. A believer in God is likely to feel closer to him through prayer, especially when they take time to listen to him as well as speak to him. Prayer can take many forms.

- Adoration and worship – praising God for his greatness.

- Intercession – asking God to meet the needs of others.

- Penitence – asking for forgiveness.

- Petition – asking for something from God.

Prayers may be private and individual, or they may be corporate – when a number of people pray the same prayer together. They may be formal, such as the Lord's Prayer, or spontaneous, when people make up a prayer to meet a particular need. In Islam, worshippers make special preparations to pray by washing themselves to make sure they are clean (known as wudu). Prayers (salah) are said five times a day, as well as private prayer. Muslims kneel on prayer mats as a sign of respect and pray facing in the direction of the Ka'bah in Makkah.

In most cases a person prays because they already believe in God's existence. On some occasions, however, people may come to believe in God because someone has told them about a prayer that was answered or they may just try for themselves to see if a prayer might meet a need. If it does, or if in some way they believe that God has heard and answered the prayer, they may feel they have good reasons to believe in God for themselves.

key idea

Arguments that use the existence of the natural world and its characteristics to prove the existence of God are called arguments from natural theology.

The world around us

The existence of the world and its special features is often used by religious believers to support their belief in God. Their argument essentially follows these lines.

- Nothing can come into existence on its own; everything needs a cause.

- The universe must therefore need a cause.

- Only God could be powerful enough to bring the universe into existence and keep it going.

- Therefore, God exists.

This is called an argument from **causation**. It depends on us accepting as true the fact that everything is caused by something else. If we could prove that the universe could bring itself into existence, then we could not use the existence of the universe to prove the existence of God. As things stand, there is still not enough agreement between scientists to lead to this conclusion, so arguments for the existence of God based on the world and its features continue to be popular.

Within Islam, the causation argument is known as the Kalam Argument. It was devised by two Arabic philosophers, Al-Kindi and Al-Ghazali, and begins with the fact that the world exists, then asks how it came into existence.

- Everything that begins to exist has a cause for its existence.

- The universe began to exist.

- Therefore the universe has a cause for its existence.

The features of the universe, as well as the existence of the universe, lead some people to believe in God or confirm for them that an all-powerful God must exist. One feature is that of design. When we describe something as being 'designed', we usually mean that it has a purpose of some kind – a function that someone designed and made it for. To fulfil that function, all the parts of the object have to be put together in the right order, be the right size and be made of the right materials. If this does not happen, it will not work – it will not fulfil its function. When we use something that has been designed, we are using something that has been designed and made by a person rather than by nothing, or by luck or chance. Here is an outline of the **design argument**.

- Things that are designed have been designed by someone who has used intelligence and thought.

- The universe appears to have been designed.

- Someone with intelligence and thought must have designed the universe.

- Only God could design something as complex as the universe.

- Therefore God exists.

This is a very popular reason offered by some people for believing in God. The 'design' argument encourages us to look closely at the universe and its attributes, and to think about whether it is more or less likely that they have come about by chance rather than having been created by a loving and intelligent God. Beautiful things in the universe and things that are not necessary for human beings to survive are said to need a special explanation. After all, why would they exist unless someone had specially created them? This being is thought by religious believers to be God.

did you know?

The existence of the universe provides a very old argument for the existence of God. In Christianity it is associated most often with the philosopher Thomas Aquinas.

did you know?

A similar form of the argument from causation is found in Islam, where it is called the Kalam Argument.

The complexity of a watch may be thought to reflect the complexity of the natural world

The meaning of life

Some people have come to believe in God as the result of a long search for meaning and purpose to life. They may need answers to the following questions.

- Why is human life short and sometimes unpleasant?

- Why do people suffer and die?

- What should we be doing with our lives?

- Is there a reason why we exist?

- How should I relate to others?

- Why are we limited in what we can achieve in this life?

- Will good overcome evil?

- What things have real value? Drugs? Money? Sex? Love?

It is likely that most people think about these questions (and others like them) at some point in their lives. For some people the only possible answer lies in the existence of God, without whom life may be thought to be meaningless. The physical world and human life are short and limited, so if humans find meaning in them alone, the meaning they find is also limited. God is thought to be unlimited, so those who find meaning in him will still believe that there is some significance to life and human existence, even if other things let them down. This is a hard thing to do and requires the believer to trust in God more than in themselves or the world. Because God cannot be seen or touched, this is a real test of faith. Both Christians and Muslims place great emphasis on the need for faith. Faith is tested in many ways, but that is to be expected, and for the Muslim, being able to deal with tests without losing faith is essential if a person is to be a true Muslim.

Religion in the world

Some religious believers may claim that the very fact there are so many people in the world who believe in God is a good reason to accept that he exists. The existence of religion in the world also supports their belief, because it unites them with fellow believers who share the same experience of the world as a place in which they can have a relationship with God and worship him. Although different religions suggest different ways of coming into a relationship with God, it could be said that the likelihood of God's existence increases the more people there are who believe in him, even if what they believe is not the same as everyone else.

Although religious belief is often said to lead to divisions and even wars, it can also lead to great unity among people who might otherwise have nothing in common. People are often prepared to go to great lengths and make great sacrifices to help others and to try to overcome evil in God's name, for example:

- travelling to distant countries
- changing their lifestyle
- giving up everything except the bare essentials
- facing great danger.

Although many people choose to do these things for reasons other than a belief in God – care for their fellow humans or the planet, for example – it may be thought to be good evidence for God's existence that people are prepared to do things at great cost and inconvenience to themselves because they believe that by doing so they are being obedient to him.

Atheism and agnosticism

Despite all the different types of apparent evidence for God's existence that give religious believers a reason for their faith, there are still many people who do not believe in God. They may consider themselves to be **agnostics** or **atheists**.

Agnosticism

An agnostic claims that since there is no completely reliable evidence for either the existence or non-existence of God, then the only possible position to maintain is that of 'not knowing'. In principle, an agnostic will be open to believing in God if they discover evidence that they consider to be reliable and convincing. In the same way, an agnostic who experiences great suffering or who hears a new argument against the existence of God might become an atheist if they feel that it provides the decisive evidence they have been looking for. In the meantime, they will hold back from making a decision either in favour of God's existence or against it.

Atheism

Atheism is the word used to describe non-belief in God, and an atheist is someone who does not believe in God's existence. Like belief in God, there are many reasons why people may be atheists. One common reason may be that the religious explanations of the world that we have looked at are not convincing to everyone. While someone who believes in God may argue that God is the best explanation for the existence of the universe and its features, an atheist may claim there is no proof of this. On the other hand, scientific discoveries have taught us a great deal about the world and offered theories about its origin that seem to some to be far more convincing. Because scientific theories are accompanied by **empirical evidence** of some kind – that is, evidence that can be confirmed by use of the senses – they carry a lot of weight. Things that can be seen, heard, smelt or touched contribute very powerfully to the way people interpret the world, since they are usually thought to give a good idea of what is *real*. When things can't be seen, it is

key idea

If we put together more than one reason why people believe in God, we have what is called a **cumulative argument**. This is an argument with more than one element to it, so it can be more convincing than one reason or argument on its own.

key idea

Allah's Apostle said:'*Whoever possesses the (following) three qualities will have the sweetness of faith: (1) the one to whom Allah and His Apostle becomes dearer than anything else; (2) who loves a person and he loves him only for Allah's Sake; (3) who hates to revert to atheism (disbelief) as he hates to be thrown into the Fire.*' (Al-Bukhari, Vol.1 Hadith 15) harder to pin down whether they are true or not. This is where faith comes in, and an atheist may claim that it is not sensible to believe in something that can't be verified by the senses.

Within Islam, negation or denial (At Ta'teel) of God could take a number of different forms:

- denying the perfection of God, his names or attributes

- failing to worship him or worshiping others along with him

- denying the relationship between creation and God, such as claiming that the universe has no beginning, and that it has always and will always work according to its own internal rules, without the need for God.

Non-religious explanations of the universe

Scientific explanations of the universe include theories such as the Big Bang and Natural Selection.

The Big Bang

This theory suggests that the universe came about through an explosion of matter and energy some 15 billion years ago. It also suggests that what existed beforehand is completely unknown and a matter of pure speculation. An atheist may argue that if a religious believer claims that God existed before the explosion and perhaps in some way brought it about, they are basing that claim on something that cannot be proven and so can have no real value.

Natural Selection

This theory was popularized in the nineteenth century by Charles Darwin, who argued that all living things have descended from common ancestors and that each generation has adapted or evolved from more primitive forms of life. The earth itself is also in a process of evolution or change. Religious believers who reject this theory do so because it seems to eliminate the need for God. Rather than living things being created fully formed, they gradually evolve from chemical matter and needed no personal, divine action.

The problem of miracles

Although miracles are considered by religious believers to offer convincing evidence for the existence of God, some might think they actually support atheism. This is because there could be other good, or even better, explanations for what appears to be a miracle. Sometimes a person may recover unexpectedly from an illness. While a religious believer may claim this is because God has performed a miracle, it could be explained naturally or medically. Lucky events can be thought of simply as coincidences rather than as God intervening in people's lives. Sometimes, people who claim to be able to perform miracles through God's power are not very reliable. They may be making such claims in order to encourage people to give money or to put their faith in the power of a human being rather than in God.

did you know?

Many nineteenth-century Christians were upset by Darwin's theory of Natural Selection because it traced human origins back to primates, which seemed to directly contradict the creation story in Genesis 1–2.

beware

Do not make the mistake of suggesting that all religious believers reject scientific theories of the origins of the universe. Many consider them to be perfectly compatible with religious belief.

Unanswered prayer

Prayers that go unanswered might lead people away from a belief in God. An atheist may claim that if a loving God exists, then unanswered prayers are a real problem, since surely he should answer the prayers of all those who pray in faith and who truly believe. It may even be possible to claim that a truly good God would answer the prayers of anyone who prayed, not just those who believe in him. Unanswered prayers test the faith of believers too. It seems natural for anyone who has prayed sincerely to ask 'Why not?' when God appears to have said 'No' to their requests.

The problem of evil

One of the strongest reasons given for atheism is the problem of evil. This ties up closely with what religious believers claim to be true about the nature of God. The problem can be expressed as follows.

- God is thought to be all-loving (**benevolent**), all-powerful (**omnipotent**) and **all-knowing** (**omniscient**).

- If God is benevolent, he would want to remove evil and suffering.

- If God is omnipotent, he would be able to remove evil and suffering.

- If God is omniscient, he would know how to remove evil and suffering.

- Therefore, both God and evil cannot exist.

- It is not reasonable to deny that the existence of evil and suffering, since they are experienced in some way by most people.

- Therefore, God cannot exist.

This is a very powerful argument, as it challenges the existence and attributes (characteristics) of God. If God exists but is not perfect, then he is not actually the God in whom religious people believe. If he is not all-good and all-loving, why should people devote their lives to serving him? Because these problems are so serious, religious believers might feel they either have to abandon their belief in God or find a convincing explanation for why God allows evil to continue and yet is still all-loving and all-powerful. This can be illustrated in the form of the **inconsistent triad** as below:

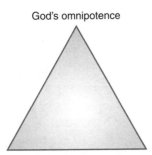

God's omnipotence

The existence of evil   God's benevolence

exam watch

In the exam, it is quite acceptable to reproduce a simple diagram like the one shown opposite as long as you explain it clearly.

The religious believer cannot deny that any of these three elements are true. The believer is committed to believing that God is all-powerful and all-loving, and it would be foolish to suggest that evil does not exist. However, together all three elements present a problem that needs to be resolved.

Traditionally, there are thought to be two types of evil:

- **moral evil** – evil actions performed by human beings, and the evil consequences of such actions (for example, murder, rape, war, theft)
- **natural evil** – faults and flaws in the natural world that are beyond human control (for example, famine, disease, natural disasters and freak weather conditions).

Christian responses to the problem of evil

Christians have traditionally thought it very important to respond to the problem of evil. One of the oldest responses is based on the accounts of creation and the fall in Genesis 1–3. The Genesis accounts suggest that God created the world and human beings perfectly, and that he gave humans free will – that is, the ability to make choices without being influenced by outside forces.

Poverty, famine and disease are all examples of suffering which demand an explanation

hints and tips

The two types of evil (moral and natural) can overlap. For instance, the moral evil of war can lead to the natural evil of famine. Human greed often limits natural resources to those in society who have the

read more

Read Genesis chapters 1–3 now. These chapters are vital to your understanding of the response of Christians to the problem of evil.

Using free will

Human beings are able to make a vast range of choices. Some may not seem to be particularly significant – for example, what we wear or which newspaper we read. Others may have a greater impact. But what is even more important is that we can make moral choices. These are choices that have an effect on other people. We can choose to do things that cause harm or do good, and when these choices are made freely they have real meaning. If we are made to do things because we are told they are good, rather than doing them freely, we are less likely to learn positive things from them or become more morally developed human beings.

The example of free will in Genesis

The Genesis story teaches that the first human beings, Adam and Eve, chose to use their free will to disobey the command God gave them not to eat of the fruit of the tree of the knowledge. When they did eat the fruit, sin and suffering were brought into the world by their freely chosen actions. As a result, God dealt out certain punishments – pain in childbirth, male domination, poor harvests and, most importantly, separation from God. Christians who accept this account also believe that God had already planned the coming of Jesus to die and rise to bring sinful humanity back into a relationship with God, so the outcome was not all negative.

The effect of our choices in life and death

A similar response to the problem of evil claims that if we make genuine choices to do good we can help humanity become better and contribute to making the world a better place. Although there is always the possibility that people will make wrong choices and contribute towards evil and pain in the world, it is better that we have genuine free will and the risk of making wrong choices because then the good choices we make are truly significant. Many Christians believe that the choices we make also have an influence on where we will go after death. They believe people can grow closer to God or further away from him, and the existence of suffering helps people to make choices that please God – for example, comforting the bereaved, feeding the hungry and preserving the environment. Furthermore, unless we know what it means to suffer, the bliss of **Heaven** will not have the same meaning to us.

Ultimately, however, many Christian claim that we cannot ever really understand God's reasons for allowing evil and suffering to continue in a world that he controls. This should not cause us to doubt his love, however, because even if his reasons are not clear to human beings, he works with a final plan in view, which is all-good and all-loving.

> **read more**
>
> Revelation 21: 4 describes the perfect state of affairs at the end of time.

Islamic responses to the problem of evil

For a Muslim, evil, pain and suffering are all part of the test God sets for humanity. Muslims believe that human beings should expect to experience some degree of suffering throughout their lives, since the way in which they respond to it will have an influence on the rewards they receive in the afterlife. Suffering should not be avoided because it enables human beings to grow closer to God, to become more spiritually mature and to prove their faithfulness to God. It is part of life and should be accepted as part of what it means to be a human being.

Like much Christian teaching, Muslim teaching also includes the concept of free will. Satan (Iblis), an angel with free will who rebelled against God, was thrown out of Heaven and now uses evil to tempt human beings. However, Islamic philosophers of the middle ages did not directly address the problem of evil. This is possibly because Islamic philosophers did not engage in any debates about the non-existence of God, with which the problem of evil is often associated. However, they did still have to consider how to reconcile the absolute unity and perfection of God with the fact that in the world there are many imperfections. If God is all-perfect and the world is a result of divine will, we are then faced with a problem. The imperfection of the world sets it apart from God who is perfect. In the 20th century the Islamic philosopher Muhammad Iqbal attempted to address this problem by suggesting that goodness would not be possible without evil. The evil in the world is meant to be overcome. But whoever asks why there must be evil when God can remove it is missing the point, because without evil there could be no moral or spiritual development.

> **key idea**
>
> Surah 2: 155–6 says: 'Be sure we shall test you with something of fear and hunger, some loss in goods or lives or the fruits of your toil, but give glad tidings to those who patiently persevere, who say when afflicted with calamity, "To God we belong and to him is our return"'.

Sample questions

Short question
a What is a miracle? (2 marks)   Go to page 90 to check your answer.

Examination type questions

b Outline the beliefs of an atheist   (6 marks)

Student's answer

The most important thing to remember when writing your answers is that the more useful and relevant information and evaluation you put in, the greater your marks will be.

A basic answer to part (b) might be:

An atheist might believe that all the evil and suffering in the world means that there cannot be a loving God …   (2 marks)

To get more marks, you must develop your answer, perhaps like this:

… Millions of people in the world are starving, and there are many wars and unnecessary suffering. If there was a God, he would surely do something about this. As nothing seems to help, then a person might say that this shows that there is no God …   (4 marks)

To get full marks, you need to offer other reasons and go into a little more depth. You should also try and use some religious language, like this:

… An atheist may also believe that the advances in modern science 'prove' that the Bible isn't true and that there is no God. For instance, the Bible says that God created Adam and Eve, the first humans, in one day, but evolution has shown that humanity took millions of years to evolve. Similarly, a person might be an atheist because in the past, they may have believed in God and prayed to him perhaps at a time of illness or crisis, but their prayers were not answered. This might have led them to think that there is no God there to answer them. This was certainly the view of famous atheist philosophers such as Freud and Nietzche.   (6 marks)

An excellent answer to this question might read like this:

An atheist might believe that because it is impossible to prove the existence of God there are no convincing reasons to believe in him. Since God cannot be heard, seen or touched in any physical way, it is simply a matter of faith whether he exists. Many atheists may argue that physical evidence provides the only reliable evidence for the existence of anything and it is meaningless to speak of the existence of anything that cannot be physically proven. Rather, some atheists may suggest that there is actually more evidence that counts against the existence of God – evil, pain and suffering are often considered to be the biggest obstacles to belief in a loving and powerful God. Also, religious explanations of the universe may be considered to be less convincing than scientific explanations that appear to have the benefit of physical proof. Finally, some atheists may believe that religion and belief in God serve only to support the weak, and that psychologically strong people have no need for God and so do not need to invent him to help them cope with the world.   (6 marks)

c Explain how the appearance of design and order in the world may lead to or support belief in God.   (8 marks)

Student's answer

Many Christians claim that the natural world contains many features that can only be satisfactorily explained by belief in God. The world appears to have been designed – that is, that its parts have been put together to fulfil a purpose and that everything happens in the order necessary to bring about the best outcome. For example, the seasons always occur in the same order and things appropriate to the seasons happen at a predictable time. Birds migrate when the weather is cold; flowers bloom when the sun shines; and camels are able to conserve reserves of water to sustain them through the desert. It may be that these things have come about through chance and that they are a matter of random luck. Religious believers, however, are more likely to claim that they are the work of God, who has designed everything according to a perfect order. They may also add that the world contains many things that are beautiful and that beauty is a personal thing, better explained as being the work of a personal God rather than the result of chance.

The fact that the universe exists at all could also be thought to point to the existence of God. For something to exist it needs to be brought into existence by something that already exists, otherwise there is no good reason for it to exist. Many Christians suggest that it is meaningless to say that something just exists — you need to be able to say why it exists. God is the best explanation for why the universe exists, since it needs a being of great power to bring it into existence. The best known version of this argument for the existence of God is the argument from causation, made popular in Christian thought by Thomas Aquinas.

(8 marks)

d 'Children should be allowed to make up their own minds about whether or not to believe in God.' Do you agree? Give reasons for your answer showing you have considered another point of view.

(4 marks)

Student's answer

I agree that it is better for people to come to believe in God on their own, perhaps because they have experienced a miracle, had a prayer answered, or because they have friends who are believers who have told them about their faith. Belief in God should be something that has significance to a person's life and since everyone is different they need to have their own relationship with God. Just to believe in God because your parents do, for example, makes no sense. Would you believe in pink pixies just because your parents do? Obviously not, so why believe in God because they say so? God cannot be seen or touched in the same way as things in the world, so we need to have very good reasons to believe in him, not just the word of others.

On the other hand, it may be helpful to someone coming to believe in God if their parents already believe. If they have a positive experience of their parents' belief — not being forced to believe what they believe, but hearing about how it might have made a difference to their parents' lives, and seeing how it might affect their behaviour — then this can be helpful, but it still leaves the child free to make up their own mind. Some people do not believe in God as a child even though their parents do, but when they are older they might come to believe themselves through their own experience or reason, then realize that the things their parents said had made more of an impact on them than they thought at the time.

Overall, belief in God is a personal matter and belief that is directly influenced or forced by someone else will not have the same personal significance to how a person lives their life. However, it is probably true to say that if someone is brought up in a religious family they will have more knowledge about religion, which may help them later to make an informed decision about their faith.

(4 marks)

Examiner's comments for answer (d)

This is a good answer because the candidate has done exactly what they have been asked to do; they have given their opinion and shown that there is another side to it as well. (Remember that you do not actually have to say what you really feel, but you do have to offer a range of possible views.) It is also good because the candidate has given a rather sophisticated and philosophical answer. The idea that you would not believe in the existence of magical creatures just on the word of your parents is a really good one at this level. This candidate likes thinking about things on a conceptual level, which may not help them in factual questions, but it has been very useful here.

Examination practice questions

1 What is meant by a religious experience? (2 marks)

2 What is meant by agnosticism? (2 marks)

3 Outline the view that evil and suffering are a problem for religious believers. (6 marks)

4 Outline the ways in which a person might come to believe in God. (6 marks)

5 Explain arguments for and against the case that miracles provide grounds for belief in God. (8 marks)

6 'Belief in God is for those who cannot cope with the real world.' Do you agree?
Give reasons for your answer, showing you have considered another point of view. (4 marks)

Checklist for revision

	Understand and know	Need more revision	Do not understand
Ways in which people come to believe in God	☐	☐	☐
Agnosticism and atheism	☐	☐	☐
The problem of evil	☐	☐	☐

2 Matters of life and death

exam watch

You should base your answers to the questions in this section on Christianity and one other religion.

What do I need to know?

- What religious believers understand to be the nature of life.
- Religious and **secular** beliefs concerning life after death.
- The religious and ethical problems surrounding **abortion**.
- The problems raised by the practice of **euthanasia**.

The sanctity of life

Many religions teach that life is a gift from God and belongs to God. For Christians, life is of the highest value. This is because, according to the Bible, humans are made in the image of God himself and this gives humanity a very special relationship with him. Human life is regarded as sacred or holy because God himself became human in the person of Jesus Christ. Christians believe that this makes human life very special and that it must be cherished and preserved. This is known as the **sanctity of life**.

For Christians, the coming of Jesus Christ into the world is very important. Jesus came in order to teach humanity about God's love for them and, when he died, his death was a sacrifice so that people could have their relationship with God restored.

'*For God so loved the world that he gave his one and only Son, that whoever believes in him shall not perish but have eternal life.*' (John 3: 16)

People view the birth of a baby as very special and usually want to protect and nurture it

For Christians, the human body is not regarded simply as a physical object, it is the dwelling place of the Holy Spirit, which comes from God and therefore must always be treated with reverence and respect.

'*Your body is a temple of the Holy Spirit, who is in you, whom you have received from God? You are not on your own … therefore honour God with your body.*' (1 Corinthians 6: 19–20)

This means that, for Christians, it is wrong to kill another human being.

'*You shall not murder.*' (Exodus 20: 13)

Only God should have control over life's beginning and its end – once God has created life, only he has the right to bring it to an end.

In Islam too, life is sacred because God has created it, and to violate the holiness of life is a serious sin. God alone calls life into being and deals out death. Birth is seen as a great gift from God and death as something that occurs only according to his command.

key ideas

'*So God created man in his own image, in the image of God he created him; male and female he created them.*' (Genesis 1: 27)

'*If we live, we live to the Lord; and if we die, we die to the Lord. So, whether we live or die, we belong to the Lord.*' (Romans 14: 8)

'*God alone is the Lord of life … no one can under any circumstances claim for himself the right directly to destroy an innocent human being.*' (Catechism of the Catholic Church)

Life after death

The question of whether or not there is life after death is one of the greatest mysteries. There are many different viewpoints held both by religious believers and by non-believers. The question revolves around what, if anything, survives death and whether what survives is really us.

Why do people believe in life after death?

All physical life ends. Yet for many people (not just religious believers) this is hard to accept. So the idea that there might be a life after death is very desirable. There are many reasons for this, which may be shared by religious believers in all traditions.

- It is difficult to believe that this life is all there is. People might feel there ought to be something beyond earthly life – something that gives meaning to life.

- Earthly life is short. An afterlife might be the place where humanity could fulfil its potential.

- Many people might feel that there should be a reward for those who lead good lives on earth and, possibly, punishment for those who have been evil.

- If life is sacred and of high value, perhaps it ought to carry on beyond death.

What Christianity teaches

The Bible speaks of God's unending love for his people, a love that continues beyond death. For Christians, the death and resurrection of Jesus Christ are proof that there is life beyond the grave. For them, it is a message of hope that, while earthly life is short, it is preparation for eternal life with God. However, Christians themselves differ in their views about life after death, although most tend to accept one of these concepts:

- immortality of the soul

- bodily resurrection.

Immortality of the soul

This is the belief that humans have a physical body and a spiritual, **immortal soul**, which is their real self. Some Christians believe that the soul survives the death of the physical body and goes on to exist in a spiritual realm, such as Heaven. According to this view, when death occurs, the soul goes before God and is judged. After this, the views of Christians differ. Some say that, after judgement, those who have accepted Jesus and lived according to his teachings will enter Heaven and be with God forever, while everyone else will go to **Hell**.

However, such a viewpoint does have problems. The most crucial one is whether or not the immortal soul is really a person. One might argue that a person without a body is not a person at all. Are there, for instance, male and female souls? This leads on to the question of where souls actually go when the body dies. Thomas Aquinas (see Chapter 1) suggested three possible places.

- Hell – a place of eternal punishment for the worst people.

- **Purgatory** – a place where Christians who have lapsed in their faith may undergo a period of punishment and purification.

exam watch

Quotations from the Bible, the Qur'an or other religious texts are a very good way of showing the examiner that you have studied in depth and understand how the original material relates to the topics on the specification.

key idea

The idea of having a physical body and an immortal soul is known as **dualism** since it rests on the belief that there are two parts to human nature – the physical and the spiritual.

- Beatific vision – Heaven: a place of everlasting joy and happiness, where God dwells. This is the eternal home for faithful Christians and those who have completed Purgatory.

'Those who have died in God's grace and are perfectly purified go to Heaven. Those who have died in God's grace but were imperfectly purified [for example, Catholic sinners] *will go to Purgatory and be purified. Those who have refused to believe will go to Hell. Then Jesus will come back to earth, the dead will be raised and all these souls will be reunited with their bodies. Then God will judge everyone. A new Heaven and earth will be made and the resurrected from Heaven will live there forever, but the resurrected from Hell will return there forever.'* (Catechism of the Catholic Church)

A depiction of Hell (Jahannam)

However, many people, including a number of Christians, do not believe in Hell – saying that an all-powerful, loving God could not allow such a place to exist. Moreover, they claim eternal life should be available to all humanity, not just to Christians.

The doctrine of the **communion of saints** encapsulates the belief that Christians who have died and gone to Heaven are part of the Christian community on earth as well. Some Christians believe that it is possible to pray to Christians (the Saints) in Heaven to ask for their help and guidance.

Bodily resurrection

The doctrine of bodily resurrection suggests that, by an act of God's love, the dead will one day be restored to life again in bodily form. When a person dies, that is the end of their life; there is no soul that lives on. However, at a future date, there will be the Day of Judgement, when the dead will be raised and God will judge the world. Evil will be banished forever and the righteous will be rewarded with eternal life.

'God "will give to each person according to what he has done". To those who by persistence in doing good seek glory, honour and immortality, he will give eternal life.' (Romans 2: 6–7)

Bodily resurrection is not the same as resuscitating a corpse. God recreates the person on the Day of Judgement, but this time their body is spiritual and will never die. This is shown most clearly by the resurrection of Jesus Christ himself, who appears to the disciples after his death. He talks to them, eats with them and they can touch him.

Read Revelation 20: 11–15 for a graphic description of the events at the end of time.

read more

'Look at my hands and my feet. It is I myself! Touch me and see; a ghost does not have flesh and bones, as you see I have.' (Luke 24: 39)

Later in the New Testament, Paul explains that the resurrected body, even though it looks the same as the physical body, is spiritual and therefore cannot die.

'So will it be with the resurrection of the dead. The body that is sown is perishable, it is raised imperishable … it is sown in a natural body, it is raised a spiritual body.' (1 Corinthians 15: 42, 44)

There are interesting difficulties with the doctrine of bodily resurrection.

- If a person is resurrected is it still really them or something that just looks like them?

- If God recreates a person, what do they look like? Is it how they were at moment they died? Or do they look like they did at some other point in their life?

- What about people who have disabilities on earth? Will they still have these disabilities in eternal life?

- Where do all these bodies live? What about the problem of overcrowding?

What Islam teaches

Belief in Al-Akhira, life after death, is so crucial to the Islamic faith that to doubt it amounts to the denial of God himself. Islam teaches that after death, the body remains in the grave until the time comes for it to be judged and thereafter sent to Paradise or Hell. On the Day of Judgement, God will raise everyone from the dead and recreate their bodies to an exact replica of the body they had on earth. Paradise will be a beautiful place of great joy, but Hell will be a place of sorrow and torment. To avoid Hell, a Muslim must be a faithful follower of the Qur'an and the Shari'ah law (based partially on the Qur'an, on the teachings of the Prophet Muhammad and on the work of Islamic scholars). Although most Muslims believe that all non-Muslims will go to Hell, some suggest that non-Muslims who have led good lives will also go to Heaven. Graves of Muslims are treated with respect and cremation is never an option. Muslims are acutely aware that the life they live on earth has direct implications for the future, and that the way they behave is being observed by God with the Last Day in mind.

> **key idea**
> *'They will dwell therein for all time that the heavens and the earth endure, except as thy Lord willeth.'*
> (Surah 11: 107)

Islam observes that all the prophets of God called their people to worship him and to believe in an afterlife, a belief so significant that to deny it made all other beliefs meaningless. When the people of Makkah questioned whether there was an afterlife, the Qur'an gave logical arguments in its favour:

'Who can give life to dry bones and decomposed ones at that? Is not he who created the heavens and the earth able to create the life thereof? Yea, indeed! For he is the Creator Supreme, of skill and knowledge infinite,' (Surah 36: 78, 81).

Similarly, the Qur'an states that non-believers can offer no good argument to deny life after death:

'And they say, "What is there but our life in this world?"… But of that they have no knowledge, they merely conjecture … Their argument is nothing but this: they say "Bring back our forefathers, if what you say is true!"' (Surah 45: 24-5).

Islamic beliefs in the afterlife are, in many ways, very similar to Christian beliefs.

- God has a plan for the whole universe and all human beings.

- At the Day of Judgement the whole universe will be destroyed and the dead raised to stand before him.

- That day will be the beginning of an unending life on which every individual will be judged and rewarded by God according to their deeds.

The Qur'an teaches that if there is no afterlife then belief in God is irrelevant and even for those who did believe in God, he would be an unjust and indifferent God. A just God must punish the wicked and reward the good. However, since this is clearly not possible in this life, there must be a Day of Judgement on which God will decide the fate of each individual.

'The unbelievers say, "Never to us will come the hour"… But most surely, he may reward those who believe and work deeds of righteousness, for such is forgiveness and a sustenance most generous. But those who strive against our signs, to frustrate them, for such will be a chastisement, of painful wrath.' (Surah 34: 3–5)

Muslims believe that the day on which the dead will be raised will reveal God's justice and mercy on those who have suffered for his sake during their earthly life. The Qur'an compares such Muslims with those who have rejected God, and states that the worldly life is a preparation for eternal life after death. For those who have simply satisfied earthly desires and mocked those who have lived for God, it will be too late to be given another chance on the Day of Judgement:

*'Until, when death comes to one of them, he says "O, my Lord! Send me back to life, in order that I may work righteousness in the things I neglected". By no means …
The fire will burn their faces and they will therein grin with their lips displaced.'*
(Surah 23: 99, 104)

All this should encourage Muslims to be responsible and dutiful in their earthly life. For the individual, everything the Muslim does, every intention they have, every thought and every word, are all counted up and kept in accurate records to be brought up on the Day of Judgement. Those individuals with good records will be rewarded and welcomed into Heaven, while the wicked will be cast into Hell. Only God, however, knows the exact nature of Heaven and Hell, and the descriptions offered in the Qur'an and other religious texts are not intended to be taken literally.

The final answer

Muslims believe that the Day of Judgement will bring the final answer to many complicated and unanswerable questions of this life. Those who appear to be successful in worldly terms despite their sins will no longer be able to escape the penalty for their deeds. As a result, the important truth that morality and goodness are worth pursuing, even if they do not appear to be so in this life, will be revealed. Pursuing such goals will be seen to be the only way to live if there is to be hope for an afterlife. Islamic teaching on the afterlife should, therefore, serve as an important warning to the wicked that the justice of God will prevail.

'Those who reject truth and among the People of the Book and among the Polythesists, will be in Hell Fire, to dwell therein for aye. They are the worst of creatures.' (Surah 98: 8)

The sin of disbelief is essentially the outcome of rejecting what is good and right and presupposes that good actions and thoughts lead to belief in God. Someone who does and thinks aright has a clear conscience.

key idea

Surah 56: 1–40 of the Qur'an deals in depth with the Day of Judgement and the rewards that await people who have led a good life. *'They will be on thrones encrusted with gold and precious stones, reclining on them, facing each other. Round about them will serve youths of perpetual freshness, with goblets, shining beakers and cups filled out of clear flowing fountains. No after ache will they receive there from, nor will they suffer intoxication: and with fruits, any that they may select: and the flesh of fowls, any that they may desire.'* (Surah 56: 15–21).

'Any who believe in Allah and the Last Day, and work righteousness, shall have their reward with their Lord; on them shall be no fear, nor shall they grieve.' (Surah 2: 62)

Islam teaches that moral laws, like physical laws, work on the principle of cause and effect, and those who deliberately do wrong must face the consequences, even if those consequences lay some way ahead in the future.

Other views on life after death

In the West there are many secular (non-religious) views concerning life after death. Two of the most widespread are near-death experiences and the **paranormal**.

Near-death experiences

In recent years, scientists have examined the cases of many people who have died (perhaps during a surgical operation) and have later been resuscitated. A 1982 Gallup Poll found that 15% of respondents claimed to have had a near-death experience (NDE), and a study of cardiac patients at Southampton Hospital found that 11% reported an NDE. Although some people may be more susceptible than others to the experience, no study has revealed any significant reason why any group should be more likely to experience an NDE.

Peter Fenwick (*The Truth in the Light*, 1995) identified 12 features which represented the 'full syndrome' of NDEs, including entering a tunnel, experiencing a barrier that marked the point of no return, visiting another country, meeting relatives, a life review, the decision to return, a rapid return to the physical body, and the subsequent removal of the fear of death. In this type of experience the people who died described a feeling of floating out of their bodies, then travelling down a tunnel to emerge into another world. Here they met Jesus or a figure associated with their own religious tradition. Non-religious believers, meanwhile, often claim to have met a dead relative or friend. Between them and the figure was often a barrier or gate. At this point, they were forced to make a choice whether to cross the barrier or to return to earth. Obviously, the people describing these experiences opted to return to earthly life (hence the term *near*-death experience)!

But are such accounts really proof of life after death? It has been argued that these experiences may be hallucinations caused by a lack of oxygen to the brain. Alternatively, they could be dreams or lost subconscious memories. How do we decide if they are hallucinatory or genuine spiritual? Susan Blackmore (*Dying to Life*, 1993) makes three suggestions.

- The explanation must be coherent and specific – accounting for particular features, not just generalities.

- A theory should not posit extra, or supernatural, realms without good reason.

- The theory should provide testable predictions.

In other words, near-death experiences may be interesting phenomena, but they do not prove, of themselves, that there is life after death.

The paranormal (parapsychology)

Groups such as the Spiritualist Movement have claimed that there is a spirit world beyond this one, where people's spirits live on after death and which can be reached through seances and mediums. There are problems here, too. Over the

hints and tips

It is not likely that a religious believer would accept near-death or paranormal experiences as sufficient proof of an afterlife.

read more

There is an account in 1 Samuel 28 of how the Witch of Endor communicated with the spirit of the dead prophet Samuel.

years, the Spiritualist Movement has been the subject of much ridicule. Many elaborate hoaxes have caused people to think again about whether there is any real substance to the paranormal. Moreover, you might ask: what is the point of the spirit world? Is it just to continue life as it is on earth? Or is there something more?

Why some people do not believe in life after death

There are many people who do not believe in any kind of life after death. There are several reasons for this.

- Evidence suggests that when someone dies they eventually decay and nothing else seems to happen to them.

- It does not make sense to speak of life after death since, if there is such a thing, the person could not really be dead in the first place – life after death is a logical impossibility!

- Is an afterlife desirable anyway?

- Life is about personal identity. If a person dies and has life after death in a different form – say, as an immortal soul or a resurrected spiritual body – then they are not the same person who died. Therefore, there is no true life after death.

Abortion

An abortion is the termination of the life of a foetus in the womb. When carried out by doctors this is called a surgical abortion or therapeutic abortion. It is abortion in this sense that we shall deal with here. Abortion presents serious moral dilemmas for both religious and non-religious people. The main argument concerns whether or not the foetus in the womb is a human being. There are two conflicting viewpoints.

- It is wrong to take human life. A foetus is human life, therefore abortion is wrong.

- It is wrong to take human life. However, a foetus is not a human life, therefore abortion is not wrong.

There are several possibilities as to when human life begins.

- At the moment of fertilization.

- At the moment when the fertilized egg is implanted into the wall of the womb.

- At the moment when the foetus moves within the womb (the quickening).

- At the point when the foetus could, in principle, be capable of being born alive and exist independent of the mother.

- At birth.

Until 1967, abortions were illegal in the UK. This meant women who wanted to end their pregnancy had to resort to what were known as back street abortions. These were often carried out by unqualified people and, on many occasions, resulted in infection and sometimes the death of the woman herself. Supporters of legalized abortion claimed that women who want abortions will always try to get them anyway, legal or not. To legalize abortions would at least save such women

did you know?

The Law of Moses in the Old Testament expressly forbids people to become mediums: *'A man or woman who is a medium or spiritualist among you must be put to death.'* (Leviticus 20: 27)

did you know?

A spontaneous or natural abortion is called a miscarriage.

from further suffering. As a result, abortions are now legalized by the Abortion Act 1967 (amended 1990), which allows abortion, but only if two doctors agree on the following conditions.

- The mother's life is at risk.

- The mother's physical or mental health is at risk.

- The child might be born severely handicapped.

- There is a risk to the health of her other children.

An abortion can be carried out up to the 24th week of pregnancy. After this time the child in the womb is considered to be capable of survival outside the womb. Later abortions are therefore only permitted if the mother's life is at risk.

Arguments in favour of abortion

There are four basic arguments that might be seen as favouring abortion:

- a woman's right to choose

- considering the quality of life of the unborn child

- the double effect (an abortion may save the life of the mother)

- population growth.

A woman's right to choose
Those who support the practice of abortion usually justify it on the grounds of the rights of the mother to make choices concerning:

- what happens to her body

- what happens to her life

- her future

- her relationships

- whether to have a child.

It may also be compassionate for a woman, in difficult circumstances, to have an abortion. To have a child might cause unbearable hardship to the mother. Abortion, therefore, allows women to choose what happens to their body, and enables them to choose the right time to have a baby. In other words, the rights of the mother take precedence over those of the foetus, as long as the foetus is not able to survive outside the mother's womb.

Quality of life
The quality of life that the unborn child can expect is also an important consideration. It may be argued that the foetus has the right to a life free from pain, a minimum quality of the life and the right to be a wanted child. If these things are not possible, then abortion may be the best option.

The doctrine of double effect
If a woman's life is in danger and an abortion is necessary in order to save her life, the doctrine of double effect may be applied. This is the principle that while an abortion is undesirable, it is carried out not with the primary purpose of destroying the foetus, but to save the mother's life. In other words, the loss of the foetus is the secondary outcome of the abortion, not the primary purpose of

did you know?

There are about 180,000 legal abortions in the UK every year. Most are carried out within the first twelve weeks of pregnancy.

beware

Do not use the phrase 'pro-abortionists'. Those who support the woman's right to have an abortion do so because they support her right to make choices about her life and her body, not because they think that abortion, in itself, is a good thing.

carrying it out. Under such circumstances, it may be possible to justify an abortion to someone who is morally opposed to it.

Population growth

Some politicians have argued that abortion helps to keep the population numbers down. This may be the case particularly in traditionally Roman Catholic countries such as Brazil, which suffer from **poverty** and overcrowding.

Arguments against abortion

Anti-abortionist groups – such as LIFE and The Society for the Protection of the Unborn Child – argue their case from the point of view of the rights of the foetus. They claim that the foetus is a human being and therefore has the following rights:

- not to be killed
- to fulfil its potential
- for its life to be valued
- to be fairly represented by an unbiased third party (that is, not the mother or father).

In such cases, the rights of the foetus take precedence over those of the mother, and aborting a foetus is considered to be no different to killing any other human being. It could be considered wrong to kill a foetus just because it is handicapped, or because a baby might affect the mother's life or career, or to suggest that certain unborn babies would be better off remaining unborn.

A pro-life campaigner challenges the right to choice perspective on abortion

The Christian viewpoint

For religious believers, abortion is usually seen as wrong. The Bible highlights how God gives the gift of life to everyone: '*For you created my inmost being; you knit me together in my mother's womb*' (Psalm 139: 13). The Roman Catholic Church and many Evangelical Protestant groups in particular are opposed to abortion. They base their view on the following things.

- The sanctity of life – life is a sacred gift from God and only he can end a pregnancy.
- The Bible, which forbids the murder of human beings.
- The belief that life begins at the moment of conception.
- The belief that an unborn child is created in the image of God.
- The belief that every human being has the right to life.

✔ **action point**

There are some very interesting anti-abortion websites. Do an Internet search and see what you can find. Be critically evaluative of the methods they use to convey their message. Do you think they are effective?

key ideas

'*Abortion is a horrible crime … the law must provide appropriate sanctions for every deliberate violation of the child's rights.*' (Catechism of the Catholic Church)

'*We believe that to withdraw compassion in circumstances of extreme distress or need is a very great evil. In an imperfect world the "right" choice is sometimes the lesser of two evils.*' (Church of England)

While the Catholic Church opposes abortion under all circumstances, the Church of England and the Methodist Church take a slightly different view. They agree that abortion is undesirable, but, at the same time, it may be the lesser of two evils and, under certain circumstances, may be the most loving thing to do. For instance, an abortion might be permissible in the case of rape, severe handicap or where the life of the mother is at risk. These groups also use biblical teachings, but consider medical advances, too. They argue that abortion may be acceptable in the circumstances mentioned above because:

- Jesus taught his followers to act with a spirit of love and compassion

- if the sanctity of life can be broken in war, perhaps it may be in abortion too

- life may not begin at conception

- new medical technologies enable handicapped foetuses to be identified quickly and allow for swifter abortions with fewer side effects to the mother.

The Islamic viewpoint

Within Islam, birth control that prevents conception is permitted but abortion is only allowed when the mother's life is at risk, under which circumstances it is the lesser of two evils.

- Some Muslims claim that since the soul does not enter the foetus until sixteen weeks or 120 days, abortion before that date is permissible.

- Others argue that since it is impossible to say anything with certainty about the soul, the life of the foetus should be protected from the moment of conception and abortion cannot take place under any circumstances.

In pre-Islamic Arabia, unwanted newborns – especially girls – were buried face-down in the sand to suffocate. The Qur'an expressly forbids this: '*Kill not your children for fear of want: We shall provide sustenance for them as well as for you. Verily the killing of them is a great sin*' (Surah 31: 17). The Qur'an also states that, on the Day of Judgement, aborted babies will require an accounting of the mothers who have put their right to choose above the foetus's right to life.

Euthanasia

Euthanasia literally means 'good death' and refers to the concept of mercy killing, that is, is the action of inducing a quiet and easy death. It is used to refer to the termination of the lives of people suffering from great physical or mental handicap or a painful terminal illness.

In the UK, **voluntary euthanasia**, where a doctor deliberately and actively ends the life of a patient at their request say, by a lethal injection, is illegal. Switching off a life support machine when the patient is deemed to be brain dead or in a persistent vegetative state is the only instance in which deliberately ending a patient's life would be permissible. Assisting a patient to commit suicide – **assisted suicide** – is also against the law. However, **passive euthanasia**, where medical treatment to prolong the patient's life is no longer given and the patient is allowed to die naturally, is permissible, provided that this is what the patient requests. Similarly, a patient can give instructions that they do not want to be resuscitated (DNR) if they lose consciousness say by having a heart attack or while on the operating table. **Involuntary euthanasia** is committed when a patient who is not able to express

! beware

The issue of abortion is not specifically addressed in the Bible.

key idea

In the abortion debate, the child in the womb is generally referred to as the 'foetus' rather than the 'baby'. Anti-abortionists say that doctors choose their language carefully when talking about abortion – for example, 'terminating the foetus' does not sound quite so bad as 'killing the baby'.

exam watch

The terms **'active euthanasia'**, 'voluntary euthanasia', 'passive euthanasia', 'involuntary euthanasia' and 'non-voluntary euthanasia', are very important. Do not get them mixed up otherwise you cannot be given any credit.

their views is allowed to die. **Non-voluntary euthanasia** would be committed without consulting the patient *even if* they could express their opinion.

Arguments in favour of euthanasia

Those who support euthanasia offer the following reasons for doing so.

- It leads to a gentle, pain-free death.

- It allows the sufferer to die with dignity, rather than a slow death where the patient's physical and mental condition may increasingly deteriorate and they may suffer considerably.

- It saves on hospital and medical expenses, and allows more beds to be free for non-terminal patients.

- It relieves the burden on families who might otherwise have to go to great trouble and expense to continue medical and other care for the sick person.

Pro-euthanasia supporters argue that people should not fear death, nor see it as something evil and to be avoided. If we were to feel more comfortable with the thought of death, rather than trying to avoid it at all costs, then euthanasia might be the right way to end a life, with dignity and without pain.

In some countries, most notably the Netherlands, euthanasia has been made legal under strict conditions. Here, supporters of euthanasia have claimed that everyone has a right to control their life, which should also include the right to control their death. The Voluntary Euthanasia Society has campaigned for people to be given the right to make Living Wills or Advance Directives. These are documents made by individuals in a time of good health, indicating that should they become severely injured or handicapped, they be allowed to die rather than receiving intensive medical treatment. However, such documents are not legally binding.

The real problem is that with the best medical care, society can keep people alive for much longer but their quality of life may be poor – for instance, keeping them pain-free by use of drugs may leave them permanently semi-conscious. Moreover, sometimes the only way to ease a person's pain is to give them huge doses of painkillers that, in the end, may kill them anyway. Sometimes this is deliberately done; such treatment is an example of double effect (see page 28).

Arguments against euthanasia

Those against euthanasia say that the task of doctors is to save lives, not end them. They argue that euthanasia is just the easy option and that there are many other matters that need to be considered.

- Patients in a persistent vegetative state have been known to recover. Moreover, not all illnesses diagnosed as terminal will necessarily end in death.

- If doctors are allowed to kill those who are very sick, then it is conceivable that society will stop looking for cures in such cases.

- If society allows euthanasia, then the elderly and the sick might feel pressurised to end their lives. This is sometimes called the slippery slope – in other words, if euthanasia is available there will be increasing pressure on people to consider it as an option.

- Terminal patients need not suffer a painful, undignified death. The Hospice Movement (see page 32) aims to care for such people and to help doctors and

> **key idea**
>
> *'Even though human death is an evil to be fought against, and a reality which can never be sought intentionally, it may also at times be accepted, even welcomed, as a sign of God's mercy.'* (John Wyatt, *Matters of Life and Death*, IVP, 1998, p.195)

> **key idea**
>
> In 1993, the House of Lords rejected a proposal to legalize euthanasia, saying: *'It would be next to impossible to ensure that all acts of euthanasia were truly voluntary.'*

the general public understand that there are alternatives to euthanasia. However, at present, hospice care can be quite expensive.

The Christian viewpoint

Like abortion, euthanasia raises the issue of the sanctity of life. Most Christian Churches are against euthanasia because life is regarded as a gift from God, which only he can take away. While some religious groups agree with the right of doctors to switch off life support machines with the consent of the person's family, the Roman Catholic Church teaches that it is wrong to take any action, medical or otherwise, that is intended to kill a patient, even if it is to relieve suffering. Failing to take action that may prolong a patients life is also considered to be wrong.

'An act or omission which causes death in order to eliminate suffering constitutes a murder greatly contrary to the dignity of the human person and to the respect due to the living God, his Creator.' (Catechism of the Catholic Church)

Many Christians consider the Hospice Movement to be an alternative to euthanasia. A hospice is a residential home where those suffering from a terminal illness can be cared for in a peaceful and dignified way during the remaining days of their life.

'We are now always able to control pain in terminal cancer in the patients sent to us … Euthanasia as advocated is wrong … it should be unnecessary and is an admission of defeat.' (Christian Hospice Movement)

The Islamic viewpoint

Most Muslims also reject euthanasia on the grounds that the reason for a person's suffering is known only to God and to bring it to an end should be left to him alone. All suffering should be seen as part of a test and euthanasia would amount to a refusal to accept the trials that play an important part in determining an individual's place in Heaven.

The principle of injury – darar – claims that no one should be hurt or cause hurt to others. Since decisions on euthanasia cause hurt to the patient and their loved ones both before and after the event, then it cannot be considered to be permissible. When faced with two evils, the lesser one should be chosen, and the suffering of a terminally sick individual is preferable to permitting euthanasia. Although the principle of hardship – mashaqqah – permits the law to be relaxed in some circumstances in order to relieve suffering, the pain and suffering of terminal illness are not among the hardships recognized by Muslim lawyers. However, in cases when recovery from a sickness seems to require nothing less than a miracle and there is increasing pain, treatment is not obligatory. If a doctor withdraws treatment which is clearly of no use, this is not a positive act of killing and is practiced for the relief of the patient and their family.

> **key idea**
>
> 'We believe that it is right to use medical treatment to control pain. We deny the right to legalize the termination of life by a doctor.' (The Salvation Army)

> ✓ **action point**
>
> Phone or visit a local hospice and ask for its publicity brochure. Think about the way it describes itself and its aims. Do you think it sounds like a good place to live with a terminal illness?

Sample questions

Short question

a What is meant by 'sanctity of life?' (2 marks)

Go to page 90 to check your answer.

Examination type questions

b Outline the arguments against a belief in life after death. (6 marks)

Student's answer

There are many reasons why people may choose not to believe in life after death. For some, life after death is not desirable anyway, while for others, the evidence of the senses tells them that when a person dies, they simply cease to be – nothing seems to live on. Some people go further and claim that the very idea of life after death is a logical impossibility anyway, since if you are dead, you cannot have life again. Furthermore, some reject the idea of life after death since, they claim, anything that lives on after death is not the dead person anyway. Death is the ceasing of that person's life and the end of their personhood. A resurrected version of them is not much different from a clone: they may look the same, but they are not actually the same person.

There is very little evidence strong enough to convince people of the existence of an afterlife. Accounts of near-death experiences can easily be explained in other ways, and mediums who claim to be able to communicate with the dead are often revealed to have no real psychic gifts. Furthermore, some may claim that the only reason people believe in an afterlife is because they are afraid of death, and it is a comforting thought rather than a reality. (6 marks)

c Explain the reasons why Christians have different views concerning abortion. (8 marks)

Student's answer

The main reason why many Christians, especially within the Roman Catholic and Evangelical Churches, are opposed to abortion is because they believe that the unborn foetus is a human being from the moment of conception. For them, it follows that to abort that foetus is to kill a human being. This is forbidden in the Bible: 'You shall not murder' (Exodus 20: 13). Abortion also violates the notion of the sanctity of life – life is a sacred gift from God and only he can take it away. To perform an abortion is to act against the will of God. The unborn child, many Christians claim, is created in the image of God and has human rights – including the right to live. The Catechism of the Catholic Church states: 'God alone is the Lord of life … no one can, under any circumstances claim for himself the right directly to destroy an innocent human being.'

However, some Christians are prepared to be more flexible because they recognize that there are times when it is more compassionate to allow an abortion than to insist that a woman continues with the pregnancy. If a woman's life is in danger it may be possible to apply the principle of double effect, which justifies performing an abortion if the primary purpose has been to save the mother's life rather than to kill the foetus. Some Christians may also argue that if pregnancy has occurred because of rape or incest, or if the baby is likely to be very seriously handicapped, then the woman should be allowed an abortion on compassionate grounds. Christians who hold these views may, however, find themselves facing considerable opposition from more conservative Christian groups. (8 marks)

Examiner's comments for answer (c)

This is a strong answer because it is equally weighted to both sides of the question. The candidate has given good reasons for why Christians may be both opposed to and, in certain circumstances, in favour of abortion. They have also shown an awareness of biblical material, the views of different churches, and of the more conceptual issues involved in a discussion of abortion (for example, double effect and the principle of the sanctity of life). The answer is well written and flows easily, and the shape of the arguments can clearly be followed.

d 'Euthanasia is always wrong.' Do you agree? Give reasons for your opinion, showing that you have considered another point of view. In your answer you should refer to at least one religion.

(4 marks)

Student's answer

As we have seen earlier, the more good information and evaluation you put into an answer, the better your marks will be.

A basic answer to part (d) might be:

Euthanasia is the deliberate killing of someone who is suffering as a result of a very serious illness or handicap. Christians might say that this is always wrong because the Bible says that people should not kill each other because everyone is created by God. This is called the 'sanctity of life' ...

(1 mark)

To get more marks, your answer needs more depth and another viewpoint, like this:

... However, many people argue that, at times, euthanasia may be a good thing, especially if the person involved is very old or suffering a great deal without any hope of getting better. They may want to die to end their suffering and the suffering of their families and friends who care for them ...

(2 marks)

To get full marks, your answer needs to have other points of view and an evaluation and conclusion, like this:

... Those who are against euthanasia say that it is the job of doctors to save lives, not take them. Moreover, many people who have been diagnosed as being seriously handicapped or terminally ill have recovered. The 'slippery slope' argument, which says that, if euthanasia was available, then pressure would be put on people to die, is a powerful one.

On the other hand, supporters of euthanasia say that a gentle, dignified death is preferable to a slow death through pain and suffering. They also argue that euthanasia will save valuable hospital and medical resources.

I share the view of many Christians that euthanasia is wrong. The Hospice Movement allows people who are terminally ill to end their days in a peaceful and dignified way, and this is surely a better way of caring for people than simply killing them — this really does fulfil the notion of the 'sanctity of life'.

(4 marks)

An excellent answer to this question might read like this:

Christians who support the view that euthanasia is always wrong tend to argue that human life is a sacred gift from God and that no one except him has the right to take life away. Many non-religious people also suggest that euthanasia is wrong because it is the easy way out of pain and suffering, and may be used as a way of keeping down the costs of medical care and prevent society from looking at ways of curing serious illness and handicap. As a result, society as a whole fails to grow and improve the quality of life available to all its members.

However, I tend to agree with those who argue in favour of euthanasia. For many terminally ill people, the thought of never getting better, being dependent upon others and losing their quality of life may make their suffering unbearable. They should be allowed to die before they get into that condition – which is sometimes called dying with dignity – and that is what euthanasia can achieve. Furthermore, I believe that our life is something over which we should be able to have some control, and that must include the freedom to make the choice to die when we choose and in the way we choose. (4 marks)

Examination practice questions

1 What is meant by 'assisted suicide'? (2 marks)
2 What is meant by the paranormal? (2 marks)
3 Outline beliefs of Christianity (or another religion) in life after death. (6 marks)
4 Explain why there are differences among Christians in their attitudes to life after death. (8 marks)
5 'Religion cannot help people prepare for death.' Do you agree? Give reasons for your opinion, showing you have considered another view. (4 marks)

Checklist for revision

	Understand and know	Need more revision	Do not understand
The sanctity of life	☐	☐	☐
Life after death	☐	☐	☐
Abortion	☐	☐	☐
Euthanasia	☐	☐	☐

3 Marriage and the family

What do I need to know?

- The meaning and significance of the **marriage** relationship.
- Alternatives to marriage.
- The legal and moral arguments surrounding **divorce**.
- The importance of the family.

exam watch

You should base your answers to questions in this section on Christianity and one other religion.

The importance of love

For religious believers, love is thought to be the greatest of all virtues and the one for which they must strive most. Often described as **agape love**, it means being respectful, kind and generous to others without expecting anything, even love itself, in return. Paul writes in 1 Corinthians 13: 13, *'And now these three remain: faith, hope and love. But the greatest of these is love.'* The model of agape love is Jesus, whose death was the supreme act of agape.

Generally speaking, agape love should not be exclusive to friends, partners and family, but should involve an attitude of love towards all people, irrespective of your relationship with them. Nevertheless, many religious believers place great emphasis on the way in which love is expressed within the family and see it as the ideal environment in which religious believers can demonstrate the true meaning of agape. Although we know this does not always work out in practice, it is a goal for which the family can aim.

exam watch

Questions on this chapter need to be answered crisply and precisely. Do not write sentimental answers or assume that in these difficult areas of personal morality there is ever an absolute right or wrong answer.

Marriage

Traditionally, one of the most important ways to show love is through marriage. Marriage is the legal union of two people, which can only be ended by the death of one partner or by the legal act of divorce. In the UK, there are four legal requirements that must be fulfilled before a marriage can take place.

- The couple must be male and female (homosexual marriages are not recognized).
- Both partners must be over sixteen years old (and, if under eighteen years, have their parents' or guardians' consent).
- Neither partner may already be married to someone else.
- Both partners must enter into the marriage freely, not under threat.

About 250,000 couples marry in the UK each year.

did you know?

The religious viewpoint

The biblical view of marriage is that it is a union ordained by God. It is one in which the man and the woman make a commitment to each other to live together in a loving relationship until the death of one of the partners. This is what is meant by faithfulness – committing yourself to having sexual relations with your marriage partner only. It forms part of the creation narratives in Genesis, suggesting that it was part of God's original ideal plan for humankind.

'For this reason a man will leave his father and mother and be united to his wife, and they will become one flesh.' (Genesis 2: 24)

Genesis 2 also suggests that marriage serves several purposes:

- companionship and friendship
- sexual fulfilment
- bearing and raising children
- enhancing a person's adult status (they move away from the authority of their parents into an adult partnership of their own).

Both Christians and Muslims see marriage as a way of ensuring that children will be brought up within the faith, become good examples of it and help to spread it further. The Bible teaches that there is an order within the marriage relationship in which the husband dominates over the wife. He must love and honour her and she, in turn, must respect and honour him.

'Wives, submit to your husbands as to the Lord. For the husband is the head of the wife as Christ is the head of the church … Husbands, love your wives, just as Christ loved the church.' (Ephesians 5: 22–25)

Not surprisingly, this teaching has caused some controversy among Christians and non-Christians, and it is difficult to interpret it satisfactorily in a society in which men and women are considered to be equal. It is only resolved, perhaps, if we place more emphasis on the husband's own submission to Christ. A truly loving husband would carry the responsibility of authority in the way that Jesus did – not to suppress, but to help, protect and encourage his wife.

The Christian perspective on sex and marriage
Many Christians believe that sex should only take place within the marriage relationship. The reasons commonly given for this include the following.

- God only commanded sexual union within a marriage partnership.
- All other forms of sexual relationship are explicitly or implicitly condemned in the Bible.
- A successful sexual relationship depends on mutual trust and security, which is easier to obtain within marriage.
- Children born outside of marriage may have a less stable family life.
- Sex outside of marriage may make a person more vulnerable to sexually transmitted diseases and sexual violence.

The Islamic perspective on sex and marriage
Within Islam, there are very similar and strict views on sex outside marriage. **Pre-marital sex**, **cohabitation**, and **adultery** are all considered equally wrong. Marriage, on the other hand, is considered highly desirable and sex within marriage is not seen to be contradictory to love for and worship of God. Rather sex within marriage is considered an asset in achieving spiritual perfection. Sexual desire is a creative gift from God and cannot, in itself, be seen as evil. Men and women, therefore, are encouraged, through marriage, to fulfil that desire and to have children.

key idea

'The sexual act must take place exclusively within marriage. Outside marriage it always constitutes a grave sin.' (The Catechism of the Catholic Church)

hints and tips

It is important to appreciate that the positive aspects of sex within marriage are by no means guaranteed, neither are the negative aspects of sex outside marriage. However, religious believers are usually reluctant to compromise on these beliefs.

key idea

'Nor come nigh to adultery for it is a shameful deed and an evil opening the road to other evils.' (Surah 17: 32)

Marriage is also considered to be a good thing because it enables men and women to avoid sexual temptation and committing sexual sins, and hence, it enhances the value of their worship. The sexes are separated during puberty to discourage sexual relationships developing and both men and women should dress to discourage sexual attention. Women often cover their heads and even their whole bodies to preserve their purity outside the home. Both men and women are encouraged to avoid looking at members of the opposite sex. In principle, therefore, the teaching of Islam is intended to satisfy the sexual needs of human beings, whilst allowing it to operate only within certain limits, an approach which is essentially shared by Christianity.

The marriage service

The Christian service

The main features of a Christian marriage service (which usually takes place in a church) are:

- exchanging vows committing to each other for life

- exchanging rings as a sign of the unending nature of the couple's relationship

- praying for God's blessing and help in their relationship

- worship and music, prayer and a sermon or address; sometimes the couple take their first holy communion as husband and wife.

A Christian marriage service also places emphasis on the presence of God as part of the lifelong union. The words of the service underline this.

'Marriage is given, that husband and wife may comfort and help each other, living faithfully together in need and in plenty, in sorrow and in joy … it is given that they may have children and be blessed in caring for them and bringing them up in accordance with God's will.' (The Alternative Service Book 1980, Hodder and Stoughton)

The Muslim ceremony

There are four key features of a Muslim wedding ceremony:

- a declaration in front of witnesses that the couple are entering freely into the marriage

- the signing of a marriage contract, which ensures that the bride's marriage gift from her husband (the mahr) remains hers unless she leaves her husband

- prayers and readings from the Qur'an, which are read by the imam, who also gives a khutbah (sermon)

- a wedding feast, which makes a public celebration of the marriage.

Imam Omer Musa (centre) with the aide of an interpreter, performs a Muslim wedding ceremony for ethnic Albanians at the refugee village in Fort Dix, New Jersey

> **key idea**
>
> Today about half of all marriages in the UK take place in a church. The rest usually take place at a Registrar's Office or other licensed location and are known as civil marriage services.

> **key idea**
>
> Priests in the Catholic Church are not allowed to marry or cohabit, whereas priests in Protestant Churches are allowed, and often encouraged, to marry and have children.

Choices relating to Christian marriages

The Bible does not say that everyone should marry; it is up to the individual and some deliberately choose not to do so for personal, social, family or religious reasons. The Catholic Church and the Church of England regard marriage as a sacrament – that is, a ceremony in which the Church conveys God's love and grace to believers. However, there are many Christians today who believe that the teaching of the Churches on marriage is too traditional and rigid, and ought to be changed or modernized. In particular, some have objected to the legalistic way in which marriage is seen – the forbidding of sex before marriage and the requirement that marriage should be for life, which can cause misery if the relationship clearly does not work and prevents people finding happiness with someone else who may be their true life partner.

Choices relating to Muslim marriages

It is expected that all Muslims will marry since Muhammad, the model for how to live as a Muslim, was married. Some Muslim marriages are still arranged by a couple's parents, and many Muslims marry young and within their faith. Monogamy is now considered the norm, although some Muslims still accept polygamy (more than one marriage partner).

Other aspects of Muslim marriages

Some versions of Shari'ah law require that married or divorced people found guilty of Zina (adultery) should be executed by stoning. Countries that are predominately Muslim or that have a large minority of Muslims vary greatly in their treatment of people found guilty of this crime. According to Amnesty International, Azerbaijan, Bulgaria, Djibouti, Macedonia, Mozambique and Turkmenistan have formally abandoned execution as the penalty for all crimes, including adultery and other sex 'crimes'. Albania, Bosnia, the Russian Federation and Turkey still retain the death penalty in theory, but do not perform it in practice. Both the Russian Federation and Turkey are expected to formally abandon it in the near future. Other countries with a large Muslim population still practice the death penalty for various crimes, including blasphemy and adultery. Saudi Arabia, the United Arab Emirates, the Sudan and some of the northern states of Nigeria practise a very strict form of Shari'ah law.

Sexual relationships and cohabitation

Many couples today choose to live together without being married. This is called cohabitation. Thirty years ago less than 7 per cent of couples lived together before marriage; now the figure is closer to 50 per cent. Some couples choose to cohabit prior to getting married, while others live together instead of getting married. This is still a difficult issue for many Christians, although some are slowly coming round to the view that a loving, monogamous, non-married relationship need not, in principle, be less valuable than a marriage.

The view of the Christian Church, as we have seen on page 37, is that sex should be restricted to marriage and that marriage should be for life. Married couples should be faithful to each other. **Promiscuity** (having casual sexual relationships), pre-marital sex (having sex before you are married) and adultery (where a married

> **did you know?**
> Jesus was not married and films that try to suggest he had a secret marriage or other sexual relationships are based on speculation, which most Christians would reject.

person has sex with someone other than their marriage partner) are considered by most Christians to be sinful.

However, increasingly Christians today believe that cohabitation should be permitted, perhaps as a 'trial marriage', and that the couple should not necessarily marry until they decide to have children. In this way, they claim, they can develop a better relationship with their partner, that is more likely to last a lifetime. In 1995, the Church of England published a report called 'Something to Celebrate', which highlighted the view that cohabiting couples should be welcomed by the Church and that such cohabiting could be seen as a step towards a final commitment to marriage.

Contraception

Contraception involves using one of a number of methods to prevent pregnancy. Artificial methods include the pill, the morning after pill, condoms, the IUD (coil) or, most radically, sterilization or vasectomy. Religious believers are divided over the use of contraception.

The Christian viewpoint

Roman Catholics are traditionally perhaps the most conservative. They believe contraception is a sinful act, since it prevents humans fulfilling God's command to *'be fruitful and increase in number'* (Genesis 1: 28). They argue that every act of sexual intercourse should be open to the possibility of conception. Protestant Christians tend to adopt more flexible approaches. They consider that within a marriage relationship, contraception can be used responsibly to plan and manage a family. The use of contraception to enable a person to live a promiscuous lifestyle without fear of an unwanted pregnancy, however, would not be viewed with the same sympathy.

The different methods of contraception are also controversial. Some Christians may argue that a barrier method (the cap or condom) is acceptable, since the sperm and egg are prevented from meeting and so conception cannot take place. However, the coil and the morning after pill, which act *after* conception and prevent implantation, are considered by some to be almost equivalent to an abortion.

Many Roman Catholics use a natural method of contraception, planning their love making around the woman's menstrual cycle and attempting to predict the times in the cycle when she is not likely to conceive.

The Muslim viewpoint

While some Muslims are completely opposed to contraception, others believe that its use is justified if the mother's life or health may be at risk from pregnancy, or that the family or new baby would suffer financially or physically. If a child would be an added burden to the family, then contraception is considered reasonable and should not be thought of as the same as an abortion.

Divorce

A divorce is the legal termination of a marriage. Until the 1960s divorce was relatively rare in the UK and was difficult to obtain. Getting a divorce meant risking the displeasure of society and many divorcees were seen as morally dubious characters. Nowadays, divorce is socially accepted and comparatively easy to obtain.

key ideas

'You shall not commit adultery.' (Exodus 20: 14)

'It is God's will that you should be sanctified: that you should avoid sexual immorality.' (1 Thessalonians 4: 3)

key idea

'That which God has joined together, let no one divide.' (The Alternative Service Book 1980, Hodder and Stoughton)

In the UK the law allows divorce if the marriage has 'irretrievably broken down' due to adultery, cruelty or desertion. Approximately a third of marriages end in divorce and the figure is rising. Some people, religious and non-religious, consider this to be a sign of social breakdown. Others see it as the compassionate relaxation of a law that held many in bondage to emotional and physical suffering or forced couples to pay a lifelong price for a single, unwise, choice.

Mrs Wallis Simpson and King Edward VIII

> **did you know?**
>
> In 1936 divorce was seen as such a disgraceful thing that King Edward VIII had to abdicate because he chose to marry Mrs Wallis Simpson, a divorcee.

The Christian viewpoint

Christians are divided on the matter of divorce. For some, it should never be allowed. For others, it is seen as a regrettable, but not sinful, consequence of the breakdown of human relationships. The Bible is not completely clear on the subject. In Mark's Gospel, Jesus appears to forbid divorce.

'Anyone who divorces his wife and marries another woman commits adultery against her.' (Mark 10: 11)

However, in Matthew's Gospel, Jesus's words are slightly different and he appears to allow for divorce in the case of unfaithfulness.

'Anyone who divorces his wife, except for marital unfaithfulness, and marries another woman commits adultery.' (Matthew 19: 9)

The Roman Catholic Church does not allow divorce among Catholics, saying that the marriage promises are vows made to God that should not be broken.

'Between the baptised, a ratified and consummated marriage cannot be dissolved by any human power or for any reason other than death.' (Catechism of the Catholic Church)

In a few cases, the Catholic Church will allow a couple to annul their marriage, which means that the marriage becomes invalid (that is, it is treated as though it never really took place). This is possible only if it can be proved that the couple did not really understand what they were doing, if they were forced into the marriage, if the marriage was not consummated (sexual intercourse had not taken place), or if one of the partners was not baptised. An annulment can only be granted with the approval of a Catholic Marriage Tribunal. A Catholic who nevertheless does seek a divorce cannot re-marry in a Catholic Church.

> **key idea**
>
> *'Marriage should always be undertaken as a lifelong commitment but there are circumstances in which a divorced person may be married in church.'* (Church of England statement on marriage)

In the Protestant Church, although divorce is not encouraged, it is more readily accepted and many Churches will allow divorcees to re-marry another person in Church. Many Christians believe that human beings can make mistakes and that relationships do break down. They argue that it is wrong to force people to stay together in a relationship that causes misery or hardship to them. They argue that Christians are allowed to ask God for his forgiveness and that they should then be free to have another chance to find happiness with a different marriage partner. Divorced people wishing to marry in church are usually required to talk to the vicar about why their marriage failed and to show why they believe that this time the marriage will last.

The Islamic viewpoint

In Islam, divorce is permitted, but there are numerous conditions concerning how the process of divorce is conducted. If either partner abandons Islam, a divorce is automatic. For any other reason, a man must announce his intention to divorce his wife three times, a month having passed between each announcement. The couple must continue to live together, but not sleep together to be clear whether the wife is pregnant, and to give the couple and their families a chance to seek reconciliation. After this period has passed, the couple are free to marry again. The husband is financially responsible for his wife until such a time as she remarries, although he continues to support the children indefinitely. If a woman divorces her husband she must repay the mahr (wedding gift).

'O Prophet! when ye do divorce women, divorce them at their prescribed periods ... and fear Allah your Lord: and turn them not out of the house, nor shall they themselves leave except in case they are guilty of some open lewdness. Those are limits set by Allah, and any who transgresses ... does verily wrong his won soul: thou knowest not if perchance Allah will bring about thereafter some new situation.' (Surah 65: 1)

The principle behind the rulings on divorce seems to emphasise the love of harmony that is characteristic of Islam. Divorce is permissible because it is one of the blessings that God gives in order to discourage harm and hardship. However, in seeking a divorce, Muslims must adhere to the teachings provided. Although there are specific teachings regarding the time of divorce – not during menstruation or while waiting to see if pregnancy has occurred – there are no specific phrases given that bring about the divorce. The intention is sufficient. If a husband takes his wife back after divorce he should ensure that he does not hurt her and that the intention is for them to have a proper marriage again. A divorce should not be given in return for money and it can only take place after the consummation of the marriage (after sexual intercourse has taken place). Great stress is placed on the waiting period after the intention to divorce has been announced. For example, if the woman is pregnant then her iddah lasts until she gives birth. It is considered to be haram even to propose to a woman who is still in her iddah, let alone draw up a marriage contract. During the iddah, she has the same rights of maintenance as any other wives the man may have, and even more so if she is pregnant or breastfeeding.

did you know?

The views of evangelical and charismatic churches on matters of sexual ethics are often very close to that of the Roman Catholic Church.

key ideas

'And if they carry life in their wombs, then spend your substance on them until they deliver their burden.' (Surah 65: 6)

'No mother shall be treated unfairly on account of her child, nor father on account of his child.' (Surah 2: 233)

The family

The way in which we view families has also changed in recent years. Nowadays there are several family types.

- **Nuclear family**: two parents and their children all living together.

- Extended family: parents, children and other relations such as grandparents, aunts, uncles and cousins all living together, or close enough to see each other on a regular or daily basis.

- **Single parent family**: one parent living alone with their children; this may be due to divorce, separation, the death of the other partner or because the parent is unmarried.

- **Reconstituted family**: where a man and woman who have children by previous relationships are married and their two families become one.

Families are united by common goals and a desire to care for and encourage each other, not just by marriage ties

Many children in the UK today live with both parents. However, due to the rising divorce rate, the greater freedom for women to choose single parenthood and the more relaxed views of society towards children born outside marriage, an increasing number are living with only one parent. Interestingly, some experts suggest that there is evidence to suggest that married people are both physically and financially better off than single people and may even live longer.

The Christian viewpoint

For Christians, one of the main purposes of marriage is to have children and bring them up in a loving Christian environment where they will grow up in the knowledge and love of God. It is the setting in which children learn how to live, how to accept authority and how to learn about God. At the time of the baptism of their child, Christian parents make promises to protect their child and to bring them up in a loving way. The Bible itself highlights the importance of family relationships.

'Children, obey your parents in the Lord, for this is right … Parents, do not exasperate your children; instead, bring them up in the training and instruction of the Lord.' (Ephesians 6: 1, 4)

Many Christians believe that all children have the right to be brought up in a loving family setting. Childless Christian couples may be encouraged to consider adopting. Many Christians may help charities involved with family life, including the Children's Society and the National Children's Home. Interestingly, some Christians are not in favour of IVF (In Vitro Fertilisation – the fertilisation of eggs and sperm in the laboratory, before implantation into the uterus) or other fertility treatments, believing that for some, it is God's will for their lives to remain childless.

The Islamic viewpoint

Muslims believe that the main purpose of marriage is to raise a family, and the ideal situation for children is to be brought up in a family with both mother and father. Muslims name the child soon after birth at the Aqiqa ceremony and parents promise to bring up the child as a good Muslim. Parents undertake the responsibility to provide for their children, to keep a halal home, to teach their children the beliefs and practices of Islam, to read the Qur'an in Arabic, and to observe salah and Ramadan. Parents should set a good example of Muslim life to their children and in turn the children should look after their parents when they are no longer able to do so themselves.

Family life, the church and the mosque

Many churches try to help parents to raise their children through Sunday schools and youth groups, in which children and young people can learn about God. Some churches establish direct relationships with local primary and secondary schools. Churches also offer help and advice to families through organizations such as the Catholic Marriage Advisory Council and the Child Welfare Council.

Family life is not confined to the raising of children. Many Christian adults believe that they should look after their parents in their old age. Here again, the churches provide help and support through organizations such as Methodist Homes for the Aged.

Within Islam, religious participation can take place at home as much as at the mosque. Most Muslim women would do most of their praying at home and with the family. The home plays a vital role in teaching Muslim children the beliefs and values of Islam – for example, the principles of haram and halal. However, mosques also run schools, known as madrasahs, where children learn to read the Qur'an in Arabic. Muslim parents may choose to send their children to a school based on Muslim principles. Marriage advice can be offered by the imam and families in financial need can apply to the mosque for support out of the zakah fund.

Homosexuality

Homosexuality is the sexual orientation or attraction to members of one's own sex, as opposed to **heterosexuality**, which is an attraction to members of the opposite sex. In the UK, the age of consent for homosexuality is sixteen, and although homosexuals cannot marry each other some Churches are prepared to give a blessing service to long-term homosexual relationships. Homosexuality is still not fully accepted in society, and many homosexual men and women are hurt by insults and other prejudices against them.

The problems Christians face

Homosexual Christians face a real problem, since they wish to express their love for a partner, but feel they are not permitted to do so because biblical teaching appears not to support homosexual practices.

The Catholic Church is against homosexual relationships. It recommends that homosexuals should stay celibate and tries to support them through times of loneliness. The Church does not permit the ordination of homosexuals into the priesthood. In the Church of England and other Protestant Churches, the approach towards homosexuals is a little more sympathetic and there is a very strong Gay Christian Movement. The relationship is judged in much the same way as a heterosexual one – namely on the strength of the love and commitment of the partners.

'There are circumstances in which individuals may justifiably choose to enter into a homosexual relationship with the hope of enjoying companionship and a physical expression of love similar to that found in marriage.' (Church of England statement on sexuality)

In the Church of England, homosexual priests are required to remain celibate. However, many congregations will still not accept a homosexual priest in their Church.

The problems Muslims face

Within Islam, homosexuality is seen as being against God's will for humanity and is considered shameful and against the Muslim law. One hadith of the Prophet goes so far as to say, *'Kill the one that is doing it and also kill the one that it is being done to'* (in reference to the active and the passive partners in gay sexual intercourse). The reason for this is that homosexuality is thought to threaten the family and that marriage is the only legitimate arena for sexual relationships, with the potential for bearing children. Islam teaches that homosexuality is a chosen, not a natural, sexual orientation, and that any homosexual can 'become' heterosexual. Some modern Muslims, however, are concerned to help and support homosexual Muslims rather than excluding them from the community.

Sample questions

Short questions
a What is **re-marriage**?   (2 marks)
Go to page 90 to check your answer.

Examination type questions

b Outline the different Christian attitudes towards divorce.   (6 marks)

Student's answer

For many Christians, and Roman Catholics in particular, divorce is forbidden. This is because, they believe, marriage is a lifelong commitment undertaken before God and should not, therefore, be broken. Although a legal divorce may bring a civil end to the marriage, the spiritual bond is unbreakable and there can therefore be no new marriage made after a divorce. Many Roman Catholic and Evangelical churches would not allow the remarriage of a divorced person in church, and may even exclude them from worship and church fellowship. They view divorce as a sin that cuts a human being off from God and which goes against God's intention at creation.

However, an increasing number of Christians support the idea of divorce in certain circumstances, particularly if a marriage relationship is clearly ended and to stay together would cause the

---

did you know?

Al-Fatiha – a Muslim homosexual rights group – estimates that 4000 homosexuals have been executed in Iran since its revolution in 1979. Ten public executions of homosexuals have been performed in Afghanistan by the Taliban army.

exam watch

In an exam or coursework, avoid using the word 'gay' to describe homosexual men and women.

couple serious hardship or misery. Violence or other forms of cruelty, alcoholism or other addictions, depression, gambling and debt, may be among the reasons that could be given to support divorce, as well as adultery. Supporters of the view argue that Jesus himself, in Matthew 19: 9, suggested that divorce was permissible on the grounds of marital unfaithfulness since adultery breaks the marriage bond of trust and faithfulness. Some may also argue that since we are human beings we make mistakes, and if we are prepared to forgive people other mistakes, we should forgive them mistakes in marriage and allow them to be free to be happy with their true life partner. (6 marks)

c Explain why family life is so important for Christians. (8 marks)

Student's answer

The difference between answers that get a grade A and those that get a B or a C is usually the amount of useful and relevant information that is contained in the answer. To get the highest marks, the answer needs to contain a range of information and evaluation.

A basic answer to part (c) might be:

Family life is important to Christians because humans need relationships. The Bible teaches that children should be brought up in a loving family environment, where they can learn how to behave, care for others and love God ... (2 marks)

To get more marks, your answer needs more depth, like this:

... Christians may argue that it is an important aspect of their faith to get married and raise children, and the family setting is the best way to do this. The Bible is very clear on the issue of raising children: 'Children, obey your parents in the Lord, for this is right' (Ephesians 6: 1) ... (4 marks)

To get full marks, your answer must give a comprehensive explanation and understanding of the issue and use some religious language, like this:

... Christians might also argue that the family unit is the best place to care for elderly relatives as well as the young. In particular, many believers can receive help and support from their churches and mosques and through agencies such as the Children's Society and Help the Aged.

The family unit is important for Christians because it gives to their family a sense of belonging, not just to each other, but to a wider religious community. The family represents the ideal setting in which people of all ages can be together and support one another, and where they can worship God together. The Christian community represent one large family of which each individual family is an important part. (8 marks)

An excellent answer to this question might read like this:

To Chrisitans, family life is important because it is the central part of human existence. It is the way in which God has ordained that children should be raised. They believe that children have the right to be brought up in a loving family environment, where they can be protected, nurtured and brought up to understand the important aspects of life – including moral behaviour, care for others and love for God. Many Christians may choose to have children, believing that it was a command of God to bear children and raise them to be strong witnesses to their faith. The family is seen as the best environment for this to happen. The importance of the family is highlighted in the teachings of the Christian Church and in the Bible itself: 'Children, obey your parents in the Lord, for this is right' (Ephesians 6: 1).

Christians may also believe that the family unit is the right place to care for elderly parents when they are no longer able to look after themselves. In raising children and looking after elderly parents, Christians can receive a great deal of support from their churches and through agencies such as the Children's Society and Homes for the Aged.

The Church help Christians to keep the family together and to bring up children to be well informed about their religion. The family is important for Christians as it should represent the ideal society in which people of all ages care for one another's needs, encourage their talents, support their weaknesses and worship God together. The Christian community represent one large family of which each individual family is an important part.

(8 marks)

d 'Couples should live together first before they get married.' Do you agree? Give reasons for your view, showing that you have considered another point of view. In your answer you should refer to at least one religion. (4 marks)

Student's answer

Many people choose to live together (cohabit) before marriage — or even without ever getting married — for many reasons. For some, they see the time as a 'trial marriage', where they can discover if they really do love their partner and can live with them forever. Others believe that marriage is either old-fashioned or just for religious believers. For some, being married is simply too much of a commitment. For many Christians, meanwhile, marriage is the way in which God has ordained that man and woman should live. They argue that living together in a sexual relationship without being married is wrong because it is against God's commandment: 'You shall not commit adultery' (Exodus 20: 14).

Moreover, marriage itself is a demonstration of commitment and, some argue, this means that people are more likely to make a greater effort to resolve their problems in the relationship, rather than just walk away. My view is that it is better for people to live together before getting married, since surely it is better to honestly make a decision that marriage is not for them than for a couple to get married, trusting in God that all will be well, then find themselves in misery but too afraid to get a divorce. However, today people who live together tend to have just as complicated financial and property arrangements as those who marry, so breaking up after living together is not necessarily any easier than divorce.

(4 marks)

Examiner's comments for answer (d)

A very clearly argued answer, with both sides clearly explained. There is good use of factual and biblical material and both viewpoints are convincing. The candidate has made clear their own view in a rational way, which rounds off a well-written response.

Examination practice

1 What is meant by homosexuality? (2 marks)
2 What is meant by a reconstituted family? (2 marks)
3 Outline the attitudes to divorce of one religion other than Christianity. (6 marks)
4 Explain why family life is important for Christians. (8 marks)
5 'It is sensible for couples to live together before they marry.' Do you agree? Give reasons for your answer, showing you have considered another point of view. (4 marks)
6 Outline the attitudes of Christianity to sex outside marriage. (6 marks)
7 'It is wrong for a religious couple to use contraception.' Do you agree? Give reasons for your answer, showing you have considered another point of view. (4 marks)

Checklist for revision

	Understand and know	Need more revision	Do not understand
Sexual relationships	☐	☐	☐
Marriage	☐	☐	☐
Divorce	☐	☐	☐
The family	☐	☐	☐
Homosexuality	☐	☐	☐

exam watch

You should base your answers to questions in this section on Christianity and one other religion.

What do I need to know?

- Changing attitudes towards women (**sexism**).

- Changing attitudes towards people of different races and ethnic origins (**racism**).

- The meaning and significance of **religious pluralism**.

- The conflict within Christianity concerning attitudes towards other world faiths.

Sexism

Sexism means to judge someone less favourably on the grounds of their sex rather than on their individual and unique qualities. **Equality** means treating people in the same way, regardless of their sex or indeed any other aspect that may be used to set them apart – for example, sexual orientation (heterosexuality/homosexuality), race, social class, education or disability.

In the UK, women have always had the right to own property and earn money, but they have not always enjoyed the same rights as men in other aspects of life. Until relatively modern times, it was believed that the role of women was to stay at home and look after the children. For instance, in 1900 only 15 per cent of married women went out to work and many employers would not employ a married woman even if she wanted to work. It was not until the two world wars that attitudes began to change. Women had to do men's jobs while the men were away – and they did them very well. Since then, various women's movements have campaigned for equal rights with men. Famous landmarks include:

- the Representation of the People Act of 1918, as a result of which women aged 31 and over could vote

- the Electoral Reform Act of 1928, as a result of which women over 21 were allowed to vote and stand as Members of Parliament (MPs)

- the Equal Pay Act of 1970, as a result of which women were given equal pay with men in same jobs

- the Sex Discrimination Act of 1975, as a result of which it became illegal to discriminate in jobs on grounds of sex.

Suffragettes campaigning for equal rights for women

Equality of education, employment and social opportunities is now virtually taken for granted, but though sexism is now illegal it does not mean that it has ended. Many women feel that there is a bias towards men at work, at home and in society, and that the fight for equality is not yet over. Other women feel that this case is overstated, and that they clearly have the same rights and opportunities as men. The different cultures we live in have a considerable influence on whether we believe that the sexes are treated equally. The predominant religious views of that culture will often be closely associated with the way in which the sexes are viewed.

The Christian viewpoint

In recent times many people, including a number of feminist scholars, have argued that the Bible comes from an age that was dominated by masculine themes and ideas and does not offer enough to women. They suggest that there are new ways of interpreting the Bible that do greater justice to women in the modern world, and which may in fact be closer to what the biblical writers had intended. Reformist feminist theology attempts to go directly to the text rather than through the history of interpretation. They read the text with feminist eyes and criticize the accepted interpretation of it. For example, the narrative of Genesis 2 and 3 (the creation and the fall) is not interpreted as a story that sanctions the oppression of women because the women ate first from the forbidden tree. Instead it is read as one of equality, in which both man and woman share in sin and punishment.

Certainly, the Bible offers varying, and possibly conflicting, viewpoints concerning women. On the one hand, the Bible teaches that men are women are equal.

'God created man in his own image … male and female he created them.' (Genesis 1: 27)

'There is neither Jew nor Greek, slave nor free, male nor female for you are all one in Christ.' (Galatians 3: 28)

Throughout his life, Jesus treated men and women equally. He had devoted female followers who stayed throughout his ministry, received serious teaching from him, and who were there at his death and resurrection. Interestingly, while it was male disciples who denied Jesus (Peter) and betrayed him (Judas), women followers are presented by the evangelists in a universally positive light!

> **read more**
>
> Look up the following incidents involving women in the Gospels: Mark 15: 40–1; Luke 23: 27; and John 4: 7–30.

On the other hand, there are some teachings in the Bible that appear to give men a more dominant role.

'Wives, submit to your husbands as to the Lord. For the husband is the head of the wife as Christ is the head of the Church.' (Ephesians 5: 22–3)

'Women should remain silent in the churches. They are not allowed to speak, but must be in submission, as the Law says.' (1 Corinthians 14: 34)

However, in recent years the Christian Church has adopted a more liberal position in many places on the equality of men and women. For instance, the old marriage vow in which a woman promised to obey her husband is no longer a compulsory part of the wedding service, although interestingly, some women still choose to say it. Nevertheless, marriage is seen as a union of equals as the Roman Catholic Marriage Service suggests.

'May her husband put his trust in her and recognize that she is his equal and the heir with him to the life of grace.'

The ordination of women

One of the greatest changes has been the ordination of women into the priesthood in the Church of England. Many denominations have ordained women into the ministry for many years, but until a few years ago, women were not permitted to become priests in the Anglican Church, a position based on the teaching of Paul.

'A woman should learn in quietness and full submission. I do not permit a woman to teach or to have authority over a man; she must be silent.' (1 Timothy 2: 11–12)

However, this was changed in 1994 when the first women were fully ordained into the priesthood of the Church of England. There are still those who feel strongly against the ordination of women to the priesthood and some individual churches will not accept women priests. The decision to open up full ordination to women caused considerable division in Christian communities. Many people chose to leave the Church of England and become members of the Roman Catholic Church, which still will not permit women to become priests.

'The Lord Jesus chose men to form the twelve apostles and the apostles did the same when they chose their successors … For this reason the ordination of women is not possible.' (Catechism of the Catholic Church)

The advantages of a gender balance

Christians in favour of having women as priests and ordained ministers often argue that it is not just an issue of equality. While women and men are fundamentally equal, each also has different skills that they can offer to their congregations. It may be, for example, that women are especially able to offer compassionate, loving and sympathetic care to people who are suffering. What's more, because some people see men as being figures of authority and may be quite afraid of men in leadership positions, they may actually relate better to a female minister. The needs of the congregation, therefore, are perhaps better met by having both men and women in leadership in the church.

The ordination of women is now permitted within the Church of England

The Islamic viewpoint

Many Muslims believe that men and women are equal in matters of religion and education, and that every instruction given in it applies equally to male and female Muslims.

'For Muslim men and women … who are patient and constant, who humble themselves … for them Allah has prepared forgiveness and a great reward.' (Surah 33: 35)

Muslims believe that men and women were created equally from the same soul and share the same rights and responsibilities.

The role of the woman at the heart of the family is considered to be very important within Islam, and her role is crucial in bringing up children as well-informed

Muslims in a halal home. While men and boys worship in the Mosque, women pray at home, based on the tradition that separating men and women for worship minimizes distractions to both. Men are given *'a degree of advantage'* (Surah 2: 228) over women because they bear the ultimate responsibility for providing for the family. Hence, a woman can only inherit half of what a man inherits, and the man has the right to take the initiative in divorce proceedings. Although women can work, they have the right to be provided for, and even if the women is wealthier than her husband he still has a duty to care for her.

The culture of female dress in Islam

In today's society wearing a hijab, which may cover a woman's head or her whole body, remains part of Muslim culture worldwide. Most Muslim women dress modestly and in Muslim countries even the most successful business women will cover. Many women welcome this practice as they feel it prevents them from being bothered by co-workers or strangers. Some modern Muslims in non-Muslim cultures choose not to cover because it would attract attention rather than discourage it. In all cases, the wearing of hijab should be because the woman wants to please God, not because she is under pressure from others to wear it.

Muslim girls wearing hijab

Racism

The UK has long been a racially mixed society and has traditionally been a nation that has welcomed and offered asylum to those suffering persecution abroad, such as Jews during the Second World War. Following the end of the British Empire, the UK government allowed widescale immigration of citizens from Commonwealth countries to live and work in the country. Many people came from different **racial** and ethnic (belief and culture) groups. Britain is, therefore, a **multi-racial** and **multi-ethnic** society.

However, this has not been without problems. Racism is the belief that some races are biologically superior to others. Indeed, many white people in the 1950s and 1960s regarded the new Commonwealth citizens with suspicion, fearing they would take white people's houses and jobs. This is called racial **prejudice**. As a result, many immigrants had to settle for the lowest-paid jobs and had to live in the poorest areas. This is **racial discrimination**, treating people less favourably because of their racial or ethnic origins.

To combat the problems of racism and to produce peace between the races (**racial harmony**) the government passed the Race Relations Act in 1976, which made it unlawful to discriminate against anyone because of race, colour, ethnic or national origin in the sphere of jobs, housing, education and welfare services. It was also illegal to incite (stir up) the public to racial hated, either in speeches or in print. Alongside the Act, the government set up the Commission for Racial Equality to fight racism and to help people understand the importance of giving everyone an equal opportunity.

The struggle with racism

Deep-seated beliefs about racial difference go back a very long way and although racism (like sexism) is illegal, almost all societies continue to struggle with it. Claims that the police, the press, employers, educational establishments and social groups are racist continue to be made, and sometimes there is evidence to support this. Other times the view reflects the fear of racism rather than the reality of it. Although the experience of most non-whites born and brought up in the UK is now one of equality, their parents and grandparents may remember less tolerant times in this country and believe that fundamental attitudes to different races are still prejudicial. Employing one or two non-white workers, or an advertisement that features a single black or Asian person in a crowd of whites is sometimes called **tokenism** (that is, including a minority figure just to ensure that there can be no claim of racism). This can be just as irritating to non-whites as overt racism.

The Christian viewpoint

The Bible condemns racism and all Christian Churches are committed to racial harmony.

'God does not show favouritism but accepts men from every nation.' (Acts 10: 34–5)

'There is neither Jew nor Greek … you are all one in Christ.' (Galatians 3: 28)

Jesus himself treated members of different races equally. He healed a Roman's servant (Luke 7: 1–10) and, according to tradition (although it is not specified in the New Testament), he had a black African carrying his cross (Luke 23: 26). However, Jesus's main teaching on racial harmony was the Parable of the Good Samaritan, in which he showed that races who hated each other should follow God's command to *'Love your neighbour as yourself'* (Luke 10: 27).

Christian work to promote racial equality

Many Churches actively work to promote racial equality. The Church of England has two committees:

- the Race and Community Relations Committee, which watches over issues of racism and problems of unemployment and imprisonment among black people

---

action point

Read a newspaper regularly over a two-week period and look for examples of claims of racist behaviour or attitudes.

read more

Read Acts 10: 9–23. This is about Peter's vision from God, which convinced him that God welcomed people of all races into the Kingdom of Heaven. This was not an easy lesson for Peter, a Jew, to accept but it had important consequences for the growth of the early church.

read more

Read the Parable of the Good Samaritan in Luke 10: 25–37.

- the Committee on Black Anglican Concerns, which helps Churches to develop anti-racist programmes and gives black people greater opportunities to participate in Church.

Other Churches also make clear statements against racism.

'We affirm that racism is a direct contradiction of the gospel of Jesus.' (Methodist Church)

'Every form of social and cultural discrimination must be curbed and eradicated as incompatible with God's design.' (Catechism of the Catholic Church)

The Islamic viewpoint

Within Islam, all Muslims are part of the ummah – the community of Muslims worldwide, who are united by their faith, irrespective of their race or colour. Unity among Muslims is helped by praying together in Arabic and facing the qibla of Makkah, and going on Hajj with Muslims from all over the world. The revelation to Muhammad was intended for all races – *'Say: "O men! I am sent unto you all, as a Messenger of Allah, to Whom belongeth the dominion of the heavens and the earth".'* (Surah 7: 158) – and no race can therefore claim to be superior over another. In his last sermon, Muhammad said clearly that all humankind is descended from Adam and Eve, that white has no superiority over black, and that the only thing that distinguishes humans from each other is piety and good action. Because Muslims come from many cultures, they cannot be defined as one racial or ethnic group; Muslims are Arab, Asian, European, black and white.

> **did you know?**
>
> The reason that Jews and Samaritans hated each other went so far back in history, to after the death of King Solomon, that no one in Jesus' time would have been alive when it began. In the same way, many people in the UK have no grounds within their own experience to feel hatred towards people of other races.

Religious pluralism

As a **multi-faith** society, the UK practises religious pluralism – that is, an acceptance of all faiths as having an equal right to co-exist. In the UK, there is **religious freedom**, and members of all religions are free to worship and have equal political rights. There are about 30 million people who claim to be Christian in the UK, about 1 million Muslims and 300,000 Jews and Hindus respectively.

Being a multi-faith nation has given the UK a variety and richness in cultural life that represents different viewpoints, cultures, festivals and ideas. One of the most well-known celebrations of cultural diversity is the annual Notting Hill Carnival (in London). Many people say this should go further – for instance, teaching more about black history and black literature in schools. However, some people disagree with this and say that the multi-faith culture means that traditional British culture is being sidelined and that the traditionally British are losing sight of their national identity.

Some Christians in the UK also express concern about the effect that religious pluralism has on the status of Christianity. Many Christians believe that Christianity is the only way to be saved and to come into a relationship with God. They worry that the prominence of other religions in the UK will encourage the view that all religions can offer an equally valid route to God. This is called 'exclusivity' (the view that only one religion can be true) and some people find it very troubling – especially if some Christians claim that the only alternative for people of other faiths is Hell.

> **key idea**
>
> Remember that many people in the UK claim to be a Christian on the basis of tradition rather than belief, so the figure given opposite does not accurately represent those who have an active Christian faith.

Christianity and other religions

For Christians there is a real difficulty with living in a multi-cultural society in which all religions are seen as equal. The problem, for them, is that Christians believe that Christianity is the only religion with the complete truth. Many believe that it is their Christian duty to try to convert all people to Christianity – a belief not shared by members of other religions.

'The Church still has the obligation and also the sacred right to evangelize all men.' (Catechism of the Catholic Church)

Healing divisions between faiths

There are three different responses by Christians to other faiths.

- Pluralism – that is, all faiths are equal and all are valid paths to God.

- **Exclusivism** – that is, only those who believe in Jesus Christ will be saved.

- **Inclusivism** – that is, Christianity has the whole truth whereas other religions only have 'part of the truth' and should therefore be allowed to continue their search for God unhindered.

Many churches and religious groups have been working together for many years to heal the divisions between different faiths. Such groups include the Council of Christians and Jews, and the Inter-faith Network for the United Kingdom. The latter represents a wide range of religious beliefs and seeks to increase understanding and awareness – particularly concerning those areas in which religions share a common goal. The view that God created all humanity to have a relationship with him, and sent Jesus to unite, not to divide, them, is considered very important.

'God did this so that men would seek him and perhaps reach out for him and find him, though he is not far from each one of us.' (Acts 17: 27)

Some religious thinkers consider that all those who believe in God should aim to be united in a single fellowship, in which defining terms such as 'Christian' and 'Muslim' are no longer used.

Islam and other religions

Muslims believe that everyone should have the freedom to worship as they choose and for their religious beliefs to be respected. Muslims do not force people into accepting Islam, something Christians have occasionally been guilty of. Christians and Jews, as People of the Book (that is, people who share certain scriptures), are given special status in the Qur'an, and a Muslim man is free to marry a Christian or Jewish woman without her having to convert.

At the same time, Muslims believe that Islam is the one true faith, the final word of God given to Muhammad, perfect and complete. Because of this, Muslims do believe they have a responsibility to convert non-Muslims to Islam, not least because only Muslims will go to Paradise.

The growth of Islam

At the moment, Islam is a growing religion in the UK, and there are increasing numbers of converts from all races. At the same time, some Muslims are concerned that the effects of living in a multi-cultural and often secular (non-religious) society are not good for British Muslims. The social pressures to drink alcohol, eat non-halal food, to have sexual relationships before and outside marriage, and to have greater freedom outside the family unit can all have a weakening effect on the ummah.

'*It may well be the task of Muslim converts to interpret Islam's spiritual message to the western world, and even to help wavering Muslims, who are succumbing to the secular society.*' (*Teach Yourself Islam*, Ruqaiyyah Maqsood, Hodder Arnold, 2003)

read more

There are many websites about Martin Luther King. Do an Internet search and read some of the views about his work.

Those who fought for equal rights among the races

During the twentieth century, two people had a very big impact on racial and equality issues – albeit with different methods and viewpoints.

- Martin Luther King
- Malcolm X.

Martin Luther King (1929–68)

One of the most famous Christians to fight for equal rights among the races was Martin Luther King, the most prominent leader of the Civil Rights Movement in the USA. The son of a Baptist minister, he dedicated his life to working for equal rights for black people in the USA, many of whom suffered great oppression from whites. Despite several threats against his life, King organized various forms of peaceful protests to try to get the authorities to grant equal rights for all. His most famous victory was against segregated transport – whites and blacks were not permitted to travel on the same buses. He also led the Southern Christian Leadership Conference, a group of 60 black clergy formed to oppose racial discrimination. Towards the end of his career he focused on the economic needs of people of all races. In 1964 he won the Nobel Peace Prize and, thanks to his work, black people were given equal voting rights with whites in 1965.

In 1968, King was assassinated by James Earl Ray. He was just 39 years old, but his famous words live on.

'*I have a dream that my four little children will one day live in a nation where they will not be judged by the colour of their skin, but by the sort of people they are.*' (Martin Luther King)

Malcolm X (1925–65)

Malcolm X (born Malcolm Little in Omaha, Nebraska on 19 May 1925) was one of the most controversial figures of the twentieth century. He was the son of a Baptist minister and supported Marcus Garvey's Universal Negro Improvement Association. While living in Omaha, the family were often harassed. At one point the family's house was set on fire. In 1929 the family moved to Lansing, Michigan, but there

Civil rights campaigners Martin Luther King and Malcolm X

Malcolm's father was killed. Malcolm moved to New York, began selling and using drugs, turned to burglary and, in 1946, was sentenced to a ten-year prison term on burglary charges. While in prison, he became acquainted with the Black Muslim sect the Nation of Islam (headed by Elijah Muhammad) and was converted. After his release from prison he became an outspoken defender of Muslim doctrines, accepting the basic argument that evil was an inherent characteristic of the 'white man's Christian world'. He called white people 'devils' and claimed that the assassination of John F Kennedy, President of the USA, was a case of 'the chickens coming home to roost'. After this, he was suspended from the Black Muslim movement by Elijah Muhammad.

Malcolm formed his own organizations, the Organization of Afro-American Unity and the Muslim Mosque Inc. In 1964 he made a pilgrimage to Islam's holy city, Makkah, and adopted the name El-Hajj Malik El Shabazz. After this he also adopted views that were not popular with other black nationalists, including the idea that not all whites were evil and that blacks could gain by working through established channels.

Like Martin Luther King, Malcolm X became the victim of death threats, and on 21 February 1965 he was shot and killed. Three of the men arrested were later identified as members of the Nation of Islam. The memory and image of Malcolm X has changed since his death. At first considered to be a violent fanatic, many now claim that he was an advocate of self-help, self-defence and education for blacks.

Sample questions

Short questions

a What is meant by 'prejudice'? (2 marks)

Go to page 90 to check your answer.

Examination type questions

b Outline the attitudes of one religion other than Christianity to the roles of men and women. (6 marks)

Student's answer

Islam teaches that men and women were created equally and should therefore be treated equally in matters of religion and education. Since men and women were both created from the same single cell from which Adam and Eve were created, there are essentially no differences between them that should lead to them being treated differently. Women should be allowed to work, earn money, attend university and own property. However, Islam also recognizes differences between the sexes which can result in different roles for men and women. Because men are usually physically stronger they should expect to provide for and protect women. Meanwhile, women's special role is in the care of the family and the home. These roles are intended to draw on their particular strengths, not to discriminate between men and women. In Islam, a woman is entitled to be provided for by her husband, even if she actually has more money than him, although men are entitled to inherit twice as much as women because they have the responsibility of caring for women.

In some Muslim cultures women are segregated from men outside the family, but in the West women and men mingle more freely, especially in the workplace. There should be no pressure exerted on women by their family to cover, although if they do it is seen as a sign of devotion to God. Today many Muslim women choose to wear a hijab to protect themselves against unwanted attention from strangers. Men are also required to dress modestly, so that both sexes are protected from sexual temptation. Muslim women usually pray at home rather than worshipping at the mosque with the male members of their family. They also take responsibility for bringing up their children as good Muslims. (6 marks)

c Explain some problems of living in a multi-faith society. (8 marks)

Student's answer

Although Christians believe that God created all human beings to be equal, and that he loves all humanity equally, many Christians find the presence of other religions in society a difficult matter. The UK is now firmly a multi-cultural and multi-faith society — that is, people from all races, cultures, religions and ethnic backgrounds live and work together in all but the most remote areas.

Christians are more aware than ever that Christianity does not have the same prominent position in UK society as it did 100, or even 50, years ago, and that other religions could be seen as legitimately competing for new converts and even indirectly influencing people to think of all religions as equally valid. Because Christianity teaches that there is only way to salvation and fellowship with God — through the death and resurrection of Jesus — it is difficult for Christians to accommodate the beliefs and practices of other faiths. No other religion accepts Jesus as the only route to salvation, and Christians believe that they cannot compromise on this at all.

With the increasing popularity of other faiths — especially Buddhism and Islam — Christians may fear that some will be tempted to turn away from Christianity and that people who may once have been converted to Christianity will convert to another faith or find spiritual satisfaction in an alternative, non-religious, set of beliefs. Because the government is always under pressure to be inclusive — providing for the needs and beliefs of non-Christians — Christians may feel that the whole Christian tradition in the UK is under threat.

Muslims living in the West, meanwhile, may also feel under pressure. In Islamic cultures there is far less pressure to drink alcohol or to eat food which are haram, since they are not available (or only available with great difficulty). Furthermore, the social temptations of the West — night clubs, pubs, fewer social restrictions, fashionable and revealing clothes, and the free intermingling of the sexes — are a serious challenge for Muslims living in a multi-faith culture.

Like Christians, Muslims believe that theirs is the only true faith and that only Muslims will go to Paradise. So although they are especially tolerant of Jews and Christians (People of the Book) they still believe they should encourage them to convert to Islam. Muslims feel less connection with Hindus and Sikhs, and, in a society where faiths intermingle regularly and easily, would be very concerned if their children wanted to marry someone who was not a Muslim — although a Muslim man who marries a Jewish or Christian woman does not need her to convert. (8 marks)

Examiner's comments for answer (c)

This is a very full answer and shows that the candidate has understood the topic well. They provide a good deal of information on Christianity and Islam and explain in some depth the reasons behind the particular attitudes of both religions and the problems these lead to in a multi-faith society. The answer is well balanced and does not fall into the trap of making unsubstantiated generalizations.

d 'Religion helps people to live together in peace.' Do you agree? Give reasons for your opinion, showing that you have considered another point of view. (4 marks)

Student's answer

Although part (d) carries fewer marks than the other two parts of the question, do not take it too lightly. The difference between the highest and lowest grades may rely on a few useful sentences in these parts. As in our previous examples, the more relevant information you put into your answer, the more marks you will get. In this question, it is important to offer a range of views.

A basic answer to part (d) might be:

Religion helps people to live in peace together because if people share the same faith, they are likely to share the same attitudes towards life, have the same viewpoints and standards of behaviour, and so there will be fewer causes of conflict ... (1 mark)

To get more marks, your answer needs more depth and alternative viewpoints, like this:

... It does not follow, however, that believers do have the same viewpoints. Even within the same religion, there are believers who cannot agree with each other – for example, in the Christian faith there is a wide range of differing views concerning matters such as marriage and divorce ... (2 marks)

To full marks, your answer must include further viewpoints and an evaluation and balanced conclusion, like this:

... Religious believers can live in peace together. Their common belief in God will enable them to worship together and share with and help one another. However, this is less true in a multi-faith society where members of different religions often clash, not only about their religions, but also on matters in the wider world – many of the conflicts around the world have their origins in a clash of religious ideals.

In my opinion, religious believers ought to be able to live in peace together, since all religions highlight the importance of people loving one another and living in harmony. However, the reality is very different and the suffering caused by religious conflict in many countries and among many communities around the world does not support the ideal that religion will help everyone to live in peace. (4 marks)

An excellent answer to this question might read like this:

Potentially, religion does help people to live together in peace. If people share a faith, then they are far more likely to share the same attitudes and have the same goals, and these help people to live without conflict and work together. They have more to bring them together than people of different faiths, and are likely to have the same outlook on important things in life such as home and family, wealth, work and leisure, use of talents and what God expects people to do with their lives.

A shared conviction in the teachings, beliefs and practices of a religion will unite people as they worship and prayer together, whether it is as a country or two individuals.

However, we cannot assume that two people who share a faith are automatically going to be able to live in peace together. Within any one religion there is a wide diversity of beliefs and a strict evangelical Christian will probably feel much more strongly about how a person leads their social life than an occasional worshipper may do, yet both would claim to be Christians. Furthermore, in a multi-faith society, people need to work especially hard to live together peacefully. Sometimes people of different religions might manage to do this more than people who share the same essential faith and yet differ on their interpretation of it. Overall, however, all those who claim to love and worship God should be trying to show their care for others by living together in peace, whether they are bound by religion or not. (4 marks)

Examination practice questions

1   What is meant by religious pluralism? (2 marks)
2   What is meant by sexism? (2 marks)
3   Outline the views of one religion other than Christianity on the roles of men and women. (6 marks)
4   Explain the attitudes of Christians on racial equality. (8 marks)
5   'Marrying outside your faith lets your community down.' Do you agree? Give reasons for your opinion, showing that you have considered another point of view. (4 marks)
6   'Men and women will never be equal in any religious society.' Do you agree? Give reasons for your opinion, showing that you have considered another point of view. (4 marks)

Checklist for revision

	Understand and know	Need more revision	Do not understand
Sexism	☐	☐	☐
Racism	☐	☐	☐
Religious pluralism	☐	☐	☐
Attitudes to other religions	☐	☐	☐

5 Religion and the media

What do I need to know?

- How religion is dealt with in the **media**.

- The range and variety of specifically religious programmes on the main terrestrial channels.

- An in-depth study of one religious programme.

- A specifically religious theme as explored in one film or TV drama.

- How TV soap operas or the national daily press deal with religious and moral issues.

beware

You cannot answer on this topic unless you have done some work yourself. Do not rely on this chapter to do it for you, because the examiner wants to see a range of responses from you. There are so many programmes, articles and films you could study – so there is no excuse!

What is the media and why is it a religious issue?

The term 'media' is shorthand for the media of mass communication. It usually refers to television, radio, newspapers and film. These mass media have become a growing and powerful influence in the twentieth and twenty-first centuries, and have played a significant role in shaping people's political views and influencing public opinion. The media is often criticized for promoting a very liberal attitude to relationships, and to sexual and social behaviour. On the other hand, it could be said that the media reflects rather than forms the changing views of society, so it can't be blamed for the views that are around us everyday.

The influence of the media

Television plays a dominant role in the lives of many people and alarming figures suggest that the average UK viewer spends 28 hours each week watching it. In some households the television is turned on first thing in the morning and stays on until last thing at night. This may play a significant part in shaping people's consumer choices – what they buy, how they vote, what fashions they follow, even what music they listen to. Because it can be so influential and is so easily available, religious believers often express very strong views about the media. Some have traditionally rejected it almost entirely and exercise very strict controls over what children, in particular, watch. This has become increasingly the case as the media has extended to include the Internet, which provides potentially unlimited access to material that would not be so freely available on television or general release films.

Although the media might be seen as having a responsibility to represent every aspect of society, religious believers feel that it can sometimes be guilty of distorting the truth and promoting worldly values. Some religious believers may even think that when exposed to a considerable amount of television broadcasting, people's ability to distinguish between good and bad, or even right and wrong, might be reduced.

The media could also be considered to be responsible for encouraging an unhealthy interest in so-called celebrities – individuals who have become figures of public interest. It might be suggested that these figures are used by the media to promote readership and viewing statistics.

The media is also closely connected with advertising and consumerism, and many religious believers fear the influence that these can have on people's lifestyles. Advertising, for instance, might encourage people to buy and consume goods they cannot afford and may not even need, possibly leading those people into debt and an unreal sense of what is a luxury and what a necessity.

What can the media offer?

There are also very positive things about the media. It has enabled people to gain a far wider knowledge of the world, politics, government and cultural diversity, as well as exposing them to drama, sport, science, the arts and social issues. Many people would argue that if the media is used discriminatingly – that means choosing carefully what we read and watch – then it can play a vital role in education and entertainment. The media can also be useful in helping people to discover their own talents and strengths.

The media and religion

The term 'religious broadcasting' is often used to refer to the range of television and radio programmes that are specifically or broadly religious in their content. Under the 1990 Broadcasting Act, religious programming of some kind is a legal requirement, but it is a continual issue of debate whether there is sufficient religious broadcasting to meet the needs of religious viewers or whether there is too much. In 2002, the Church of England Synod – the governing body of the Church of England – decided to monitor religious broadcasting and received many complaints that it had been reduced. The National Secular Society, on the other hand, was apparently 'infuriated' that so much of BBC Radio 4 was given over to religious topics – even in programmes that were not specifically religious.

In 2000, the arts and media journal *Cultural Trends* carried out a study of religious broadcasting and arrived at the following figures.

- In one month in 1998, a majority of adults (54 per cent) saw at least one religious programme, down only slightly from the 62 per cent registered a decade earlier.

- There has been a shift away from broadcasting church services towards a more varied schedule of programming, appealing to different audiences.

key idea

When the BBC was established, it was taken for granted that Britain was a Christian country and therefore religious broadcasting was a key part of its programming. Today we live in a multi-cultural, multi-faith society, which many feel should be reflected in religious broadcasting.

- Viewing had held up better among viewers aged between sixteen and 44 than among those aged over 45.

- Viewers aged sixteen to 24 and 25 to 34 saw the same number of religious programmes in February 1998 as they had ten years previously.

- The average weekly amount of religion broadcasting on ITV and BBC1 has remained the same since 1988.

- The overall amount of religion broadcasting on networked channels has increased since the launch of Channel 5.

- The journal noted that: '*This research shows that today's religious broadcasting is far removed from the popular image of ladies in hats singing hymns.*'

- The study also noted that: '*It is time that religious broadcasting was regarded as having a positive contribution to make to the health of multi-cultural Britain.*'

In 2002, Channel 4 adopted a religious programming policy that it claimed was influenced by its 'remit for cultural diversity' – in other words, it could not plan all its religious broadcasting around Christianity. The channel offered a range of programmes that were not necessarily specifically religious, but that provided an insight into issues that are of interest to religious believers. These included programmes about death, evil, black theology and the issues raised by being a Muslim in Britain. A Channel 4 team even followed Muslims going on the Hajj – a sort of religious reality TV.

In August 2003, the channel presented a series of four programmes entitled *Some of My Best Friends Are …* featuring religious believers from Catholic, Muslim, Anglican and Jewish backgrounds. These programmes tackled serious contemporary issues raised within different faiths. For example, in *Some of My Best Friends are Muslim*, Yasmin Alibhai Brown talked about polygamy, hijabs and the threats made against her, and others, who were thought to be challenging traditional Islam.

Religious broadcasting: regular programmes

A number of regular religious programmes appear on terrestrial TV, including:

- *Songs of Praise*
- *The Heaven and Earth Show*
- religious documentaries.

In addition to these programmes are those that appear on satellite and cable stations.

Songs of Praise

As the *Cultural Trends* survey suggested, religious broadcasting is not just about filming church services every Sunday morning. In fact, church services are usually now only broadcast when there is a special

> **key idea**
>
> Some people object to the daily radio programmes *Pause for Thought* and *Thought for the Day* because they think it is unfair that a religious speaker should be able to speak for three minutes on air without their opinions being challenged.

Television cameras filming an episode of Songs of Praise

event – the funeral of Princess Diana, for example, or some other public or state occasion celebrated with a church service. Even *Songs of Praise* (shown by BBC1 early Sunday evenings), the most popular specifically religious programme on terrestrial television, is no longer simply a service with lots of hymns. It now takes the form of a magazine programme. One church or Christian community may play host to the programme, and the format is diverse and modern. The music is drawn from a range of religious and inspirational traditions, and includes solo and performance items as well as congregational singing.

On Sunday 7 September 2003, *Songs of Praise* was hosted by singer Aled Jones and was based in the cathedral city of Salisbury. The programme included well-known people who live in Salisbury – for example, former Prime Minister Edward Heath and novelist Susan Howatch – talking about the role the cathedral played in their lives. Indeed, Susan Howatch talked about how it had been an important part in her conversion. On this occasion, the hymns sung were quite traditional ones, which reflected the character of the cathedral and its choir.

Aled Jones spoke to people who worked for the local charity, the Food Bank, which encourages people to purchase one extra food item at the supermarket to be donated to people in need in the area. He also interviewed a worshipper who felt that he had been specially called into God's service after God spoke to him at an airport telling him not to get on the plane he was due to catch. This has led to a complete change of life for him as he waits to find out what God's plans for him are.

The Heaven and Earth Show

Another specifically religious programme shown every Sunday morning on BBC1 is *The Heaven and Earth Show*. This is also a magazine-type programme, which features a diversity of guests not only from traditional religious backgrounds but also from many alternative faith systems and cultures. It is presented in a contemporary, informal style and gives viewers the opportunity to participate by phone, email or text, and to vote on issues being discussed. For those expecting a traditionally Christian broadcast, the show may come as a surprise as it often explores New Age belief systems and invites speakers from atheist and secular organizations to express their views.

On Sunday 7 September 2003, the show ran a special feature on belief, inviting three audience groups to take part in the studio – the Holy Folk (members of traditional religions), the New Agers (including clairvoyants, astrologers and healers) and the Sceptics (agnostics and atheists). The programme centred around a MORI poll commissioned by the BBC to find out what people in the UK believe today, and around lively discussion between representatives of the three groups. Some interesting results emerged.

- A telephone vote registered 11,000 voters, of whom 81 per cent said they believed in God and 19 per cent that they did not believe.

- The growth of scientific knowledge and understanding over the last century had not lead to the decline in spirituality that had been expected.

- Religion is passed on by the tradition and the family, while spirituality is discovered through personal experience.

did you know?

A magazine programme (such as *Songs of Praise*) is one that includes interviews, features, musical items, readings and news – but more in the style of a chat show or news and human interest programme.

did you know?

Broadcasting regulations forbid religious organizations to recruit members on air.

- We live in the age of a 'spiritual marketplace', where a huge range of options are available to people.

- Some 62 per cent of people polled said they were more influenced by their own experience, while only 17 per cent claimed to be influenced by traditional religion. Interestingly, the same percentage (17 per cent) claimed to be influenced by the media.

- New Age belief systems have increased significantly in the last 30 years because they are considered more accessible than traditional religions.

- Christianity still claims the biggest number of practising adherents in the UK, followed by Muslims, Hindus and Sikhs.

- Although attendance at traditional churches appears to be declining at a rate of 1 per cent a year, Evangelical and Charismatic Christianity is on the increase.

Whatever we think about the significance, or otherwise, of these statistics, it is clear that *The Heaven and Earth Show* is a very relevant and valuable programme for people who are interested in learning about religion and faith in today's society.

Religious documentaries

Religious documentaries, like secular ones, examine one area of particular interest, the role of an individual or group, or an issue of particular concern to religious believers or those interested in religion. One of the key targets for contemporary religious broadcasting is thought to be viewers who are not connected to any particular religious tradition, but who are interested in what we might call the big questions of life: Why are we here? How did we get here? How should we behave? How should we relate to others and to the world around us?

Examples of religious documentaries

- *Everyman* is an occasional BBC documentary series that examines what might broadly be called ethical and spiritual issues such as assisted suicide, neo-natal euthanasia, interfaith marriages and spiritualism.

- *Witness* is a Channel 4 documentary series, which, the channel says, aims to encompass *'a range of stories that collide with faith, identity and belief'*.

- *Miracles* was a one-off religious documentary shown on Channel 4 in 2000, which followed the work of Benny Hinn, the internationally renowned evangelist. The documentary team had access to several of his miracle crusades in mid-west USA and followed up carefully those who claimed to be healed. It was clear that the documentary team were very sceptical, although the programme also showed how many people were deeply committed to Hinn's ministry.

- *Running for God*, shown on ITV in 2003, followed three Christian women hurdlers as they prepared for the Commonwealth Games. The programme examined the relationship between their faith and their sporting talent.

- *Soul Searching*, shown on Channel 4 in September 2003, offered two programmes about the nature of the soul, examining questions about personal

key idea

Television programmes often use comedy to deal with religious issues and situations – for example, *The Vicar of Dibley* or *Father Ted*. Think about what this might say about the way in which television writers think their audience views religious life and people.

did you know?

A documentary is a factual film or television programme about an event or person, presenting the facts with little or no fiction.

identity and the soul, and whether the soul belongs to God and goes back to him when we die.

- *Jesus Comes to London* was shown on Channel 4 in August 2003. The documentary revolved around the character of Vissarian, an uneducated Russian preacher whose followers think is Jesus. He has set up a community in Siberia where 5000 of his disciples live, hoping to build the foundations of a new and better world to come.

Satellite and cable stations

Satellite and cable television offers a far wider range of religious broadcasting than could ever be possible on the few terrestrial channels we have in the UK. The God Channel broadcasts a constant stream of religious programmes, many of which are televised services, sermons, evangelistic rallies or talks by eminent Christian speakers and ministers. Bible-teaching programmes also fill a good deal of air time, often presented in a magazine or chat show format, and featuring a small group of people sitting together as they would in a Bible study group or fellowship meeting.

Televangelism is big business in the USA in particular, representing a highly technological industry worth millions of dollars. Many people come into contact with Christianity for the first time through watching religious broadcasts that are televised all over the world. In the USA many radio and television stations are owned by churches and run highly independent programmes. While some are very glitzy, others simply televise their regular services and are clearly working on a much lower budget.

Religious and moral issues in film

Religious issues are sometimes the topic of television films. The BBC film *Son of God*, shown in spring 2003, was about a young man in the north of England who, after a religious experience similar to Jesus's temptations in the wilderness, believed that he was the Son of God. The film showed the way in which his friends, family and strangers responded to his claims, offering some parallels to the way in which the gospels portray the relationship between Jesus and his disciples. Although the film was not aimed at a religious audience, some background knowledge of the gospels was certainly useful in order to fully appreciate what it was trying to communicate.

Most feature length films with a religious or moral theme shown on television were not originally made for the television market, but for the big screen. Not surprisingly, film makers who need to justify the expenditure of considerable sums of money do not specifically target a prospective audience of religious believers. However, the fact that religious and moral themes do nevertheless emerge in mainstream cinema gives us a good indication that it is not just committed religious believers. However, those who regularly practise a faith who are interested in religious and moral issues.

In most cases the religious or moral theme of a film is presented alongside the more usual topics: romance and relationships, family dramas, science fiction and fantasy, war and political intrigues, adventures and murders. Sometimes we need to watch and think very carefully to be able to separate the life and death issues from these popular themes.

✓ action point

Take a look at some religious programmes on satellite and cable TV. What do you think of them? Have they affected your views in any way?

did you know?

Premier Radio, a Christian radio station in the UK, broadcasts a range of worship, teaching, news and magazine programmes throughout the UK to listeners in London and the south-east.

Examples of films with religious or moral themes

In the text that follows, we will take a closer look at *Yentl*, *Priest* and *Gattaca* – all very different films, but each with a strongly religious theme.

Yentl (1983)
Director: Barbara Streisand. Starring Barbara Streisand and Nehemiah Persoff

This film tells the story of a young Jewish woman at the turn of the century who rebels against the tradition that women cannot study the Torah. After the death of her father, she disguises herself as a boy and enters a Yeshiva (a school for the study of the Jewish law). There are romantic elements to the plot, but these serve to underline assumptions made about male and female roles in a traditional religious society.

Priest (1994)
Director: Antonia Bird. Starring Linus Roache, Robert Carlyle and Tom Wilkinson

In this controversial film about the experiences of a homosexual Roman Catholic priest, Linus Roache gives a touching portrayal of Father Greg Pilkington, recently moved to a very poor, and potentially violent, parish in Liverpool. He is plagued by guilt borne out of unrealistic societal expectation of modern-day priests, to which he believes he and his fellow priests should be committed, but which he finds challenged by his own priest in charge, Father Matthew Thomas. Matthew is having a sexual relationship with Maria, their housekeeper, despite the vow of celibacy to which Catholic priests are bound. However, when Greg learns that Matthew and Maria genuinely love each other and that she only refuses to marry him because she doesn't want him to regret giving up the priesthood to do so, he softens his attitude. He and Matthew, however, clearly have very different perspectives on what it means to be a priest. Matthew has a social reforming zeal, whilst Greg pushes for high standards of morality and spirituality.

The parish offers Greg many challenges. The parishioners are often drunk, undignified and aggressive, and Greg feels that Matthew descends to their level too often. However, it is clear that Matthew is well-loved and knows exactly how to respond to parishioners who have little time for theology and need a priest who is prepared to meet them on their level. One night, after facing a riotous wake in a pub for a member of the parish who has just died, Greg visits a gay bar and we become aware of his homosexuality. He picks up Graham, has sex with him, and leaves. Greg's guilt and pain are clear and we see why he takes such a high moral line with Matthew – he is simply trying to escape the implications of his own sexuality. He fights against his feelings for Graham and, though they meet on several occasions, Greg is never at ease with the relationship.

The film offers more than this, however. It also tackles the difficult issue of the seal of the confessional, which ensures that whatever a priest is told in confession is confidential. When Greg is told by 14-year-old Lisa that her father has been sexually abusing her, he is tortured with guilt for not protecting her due to his belief that the confessional is sacrosanct. When Lisa's mother finds out what has been happening she cannot forgive Greg for failing to expose the truth.

Greg's crisis comes when he and Graham are arrested and charged for public indecency and he can no longer hide the truth of his sexuality from his

exam-watch

You need only base an answer on either one film or one TV drama.

✓ **action point**

Think about whether it should be the function of a feature film to examine moral, ethical or religious issues. Should their primary purpose be to entertain? If so, does this mean that they cannot convey any opinions on ethical issues?

congregation. Matthew is totally supportive, the bishop less so, but Greg's guilt is such that he feels obliged to withdraw from the parish. Matthew, however, is convinced that Greg should forgive himself and return to the parish to say mass with him, a public gesture of Matthew's commitment to Greg and his expectation that the parish should be prepared to forgive him, since none of them could claim to be sinless. Greg is less convinced.

Eventually, Matthew persuades Greg to return to the parish and they say the mass together. The church is violently and massively divided. Many leave the service, shouting abuse at both priests. Those who remain still refuse to take communion from Greg; all except Lisa. She is the only person who can truly empathize with Greg's pain, and yet he still fears she has not forgiven him for failing to inform the authorities of her father's abuse. Lisa alone takes communion from Greg. The film ends as they both break down in tears and as Lisa provides him with the genuinely accepting and forgiving comfort that Greg needed from the parish that have alienated him.

This lovely, and often very amusing film, should be watched sensitively, since it is not just about being shocked by a gay priest, but about how the calling to be a priest cannot be separated from who the priest is. Greg is convinced that God has called him to the priesthood although this is utterly opposed to his sexual orientation and causes him terrible distress. Matthew, meanwhile, is unorthodox and confrontational, especially with the hierarchy within the church. Both are not naturally suited to the priesthood and yet both are clearly gifted in their work and cannot envisage another way of life. The film challenges a lot of preconceptions in a sensitive and thought provoking way and should generate a lot of discussion amongst you and your classmates.

Gattaca (1997)
Director: Andrew Niccol. Starring Ethan Hawke and Jude Law

This film is a good example of how religious and ethical themes can be explored through a Hollywood science-fiction blockbuster.

'*Consider God's handiwork. Who can straighten what he has made crooked?*'
(Ecclesiastes 7: 13)

These words are part of the opening credits to this film, set in a '*not too distant future*' state where it is considered irresponsible to leave conception to God and nature. Instead, geneticists engineer 'perfect' embryos: '*Ten fingers and ten toes – that is all that used to matter. Not now.*' This is a world in which pianists are genetically engineered so that they can play pieces '*that can only be played with twelve fingers*'.

The hero of the film, Vincent, was not so engineered. He was a '*faith birth*'. Born with a life expectancy of 30, a heart defect and myopia, he is an '*in-valid*', destined to be part of the new underclass, discriminated against because of their imperfect DNA (genoism), and who spend their lives drifting from one menial job to another. Vincent knows that however hard he works and studies,

'*My real resume was in my cells.*'

'*We now have discrimination down to a science.*'

It is only when he beats Anton, his younger genetically engineered brother, in a regular swimming dare that he usually fails, that Vincent realizes he does not need to accept the limitations that society claims his natural birth has put on him. Vincent walks away from his family and engages the help of a man who markets the perfect DNA of '*valids*' who have fallen on hard times.

'*For the genetically superior, success is easier to obtain, but it is by no means guaranteed. There is no gene for fate, and when the elite fall on hard times, their genetic identity becomes a valuable commodity for the unscrupulous.*'

Ethan Hawke as Vincent and Jude Law as Jerome in Gattaca

Vincent enters into a contract with Jerome Morrow, a former swimming star. He is wheelchair bound following a road accident, embittered and verging on alcoholism. Vincent becomes Jerome (who is thereafter known as Eugene), and using his blood, urine, hair and skin samples to pass as Morrow, enters the space agency, Gattaca. After a murder and a romantic entanglement, Vincent achieves his aim to undertake a space mission to Titan.

The moral and religious message of the film is clear: what happens when man interferes with God's creative work? The consequences are subtle, not least that society makes judgements about people who limit their potential and frustrate their ability to be their true selves. Both Vincent and Jerome/Eugene were victims of such limiting and controlling assumptions. Neither feels truly free, but feel determined by their genes.

Hardly a week passes without claims by scientists that they have isolated the gene for some particular disease or trait. Increasingly, we are told that mental and emotional characteristics (a religious susceptibility for instance) can be attributed to our DNA. Insurance companies are thought to want to increase genetic testing in order to identify high-risk applicants for life-insurance. More and more we are being defined by our genetic make-up. *Gattaca* explores these issues. It is useful to consider how Christians and Muslims might view increased genetic testing by insurance companies and other developments that lead in the *Gattaca* direction?

Religious, moral and ethical issues in UK soap operas

A soap opera is an ongoing drama series featuring a set of regular characters, complemented by more occasional guest appearances from characters who serve a more limited purpose. The settings are intended to be realistic, although they often represent extremes – one small area of East London, for example, in which the whole range of human emotion and experience is covered in the course of a single week! Although many TV and media critics dismiss soap operas as low level drama that suffers from never reaching a conclusion, they are among the most watched and talked about programmes on television. Producers of soaps claim that they serve an educational and public function, informing the viewer about a vast range of social, public, personal and ethical issues. If a particularly emotional issue has been addressed by a soap, then a helpline phone number is often displayed at the end, so people who have been affected by the issues can get support or extra information.

The advantage of a soap is that the producers can present an issue from a variety of different standpoints. Different sides of a moral argument can be presented through the use of different characters while the programme's producers themselves are able to remain neutral. However, most soap plots operate on the principle that wrong-doing will always be found out and punished.

The way in which issues are presented can depend a lot on the character used – for example, if a sympathetic character turns out to have a history of violence, the viewer will respond quite differently to the issue than if it were associated with a character who is already considered unreliable or unlikable. Knowing something about the character's background helps us to understand the subtleties of how they respond to crises and dilemmas. This is the way in which soaps reward the regular viewer and encourage them to keep watching. When characters act unpredictably we find it even more interesting because we are surprised by their actions, but the viewer will not tolerate this if it happens too often, making the character inconsistent and unrealistic. Ultimately, if an issue the producers want to address does not fit one character, there are plenty of others to choose from.

Example of a soap opera and the issues covered: EastEnders

This popular soap continually addresses a range of moral and ethical issues. Over the years, the programme has tried to target controversial issues, such as attitudes towards HIV sufferers, as well as deal with more common ones, such as adultery. Other issues that have been addressed, or that regularly reoccur, include:

- assisted suicide
- infertility
- bereavement
- ante-natal choices – whether to have an abortion
- crime – often fraud, gangland criminal activity or petty crime
- gambling

exam watch

You only need to know how either soap operas or the national press deal with religious or moral issues.

did you know?

When BBC Radio 4's soap opera, The Archers, was first broadcast its intention was to give farmers agricultural advice in an entertaining way.

hints and tips

Because soap plots are ever-changing, do not simply rely on an old storyline you did not actually see but just read about. Set out to watch or video one soap regularly over a period of four weeks and you will soon have plenty of new material to use.

- alcoholism
- murder
- prostitution
- homosexuality
- loss of faith

- single parenthood
- drugs
- promiscuity
- inter-race relationships
- domestic violence.

Institutional drama in the UK

The Bill, *London's Burning*, *Casualty* and *Holby City* all belong to the category of drama series known as 'institutional drama'. They are all set within a closely defined area – a hospital, or a police or fire station, for example – and the plot intertwines ongoing stories about the lives of the people who work there with self-contained plots in each episode. Because institutional dramas are concerned with social and ethical issues of the day they are useful viewing for students of religious studies and ethics. In recent years, these institutional dramas have acquired the characteristics of a soap opera, rewarding the regular viewer with sustained stories about leading characters, which often take precedence over the institutional aspects of the drama.

Issues covered in two UK hospital dramas: Casualty *and* Holby City

Issues that have been covered in these dramas include:

- assisted suicide
- alcoholism
- drug-related problems

- bereavement
- organized crime
- bullying and other forms of abuse
- hospital errors

- gambling addiction
- domestic violence
- adultery, incest and other relationship issues
- post-traumatic stress
- false imprisonment
- homelessness.

Religious, moral and ethical issues in newspapers

There is no avoiding ethical issues in the newspapers. Every day you have available to you a mass of enormously helpful resource material that covers, in considerable detail, just about every ethical and moral issue known to humanity. Like soaps, they are ongoing; unlike soaps, however, they are based on real life and can, therefore, generate even more lively debate at all levels.

The wide range of newspapers available in the UK should give you the opportunity to look at how an issue is covered from several different angles. You will

✔ **action point**

Think about whether it would be realistic or useful for religious believers to become more involved in the writing and making of soap operas. Do you think that soap operas reflect the real state of religious belief in the UK, or do they underestimate how many people are committed to a religious faith?

✔ **action point**

Find out about the ethical issues that have been covered in *Coronation Street* over the years. Remember, however, that you have to be able to write about them in some depth.

exam watch

You only need to know how either soap operas or the national press deal with religious or moral issues.

find that each newspaper will usually have a relatively predictable response, depending on its readership, political stance and the moral values it is known. Some newspapers are more open about offering an opinion. Others will present issues in an apparently unbiased way but usually include columns by featured writers who are well known for expressing uncompromising opinions. Contributions from medical, legal or academic experts will present the case from differing perspectives.

Once you have chosen your issue, use a checklist like the one below to guide you though your answer.

- Language and style – is the article written to arouse readers' emotions, to make them angry or sad, or to encourage them to do something in response?

- Readership – how does the article aim to reach its target audience? Compare how *The Sun* and *The Times* might address an issue of making IVF available on the NHS, for example.

- Use of pictures – are these designed to make the reader feel moved, inspired, horrified?

- Use of headlines – are they intended to shock or puzzle?

- Consistency with other articles – how does the article fit into the style and philosophy of the paper as a whole? Are there other articles about related issues that help show how the paper is presenting the case?

Sample questions

Although the extended writing optional questions are structured differently and you have longer to answer them, as with ordinary examination questions, the more useful knowledge and evaluation that you write down, the more marks you will get.

The questions are marked by levels. Level 1 gives the fewest marks and is for simple ideas and examples. Level 2 offers slightly higher marks and requires some discussion and understanding of the basic information. Level 3, which is higher still, offers good marks for clearly structured answers with more in-depth knowledge and evaluation. Finally, level 4, the top level, gives the highest marks for answers that are comprehensive, show a full understanding and use religious language.

hints and tips

Find an ethical issue to write about that no one else in your class is using. Do not use just one type of newspaper; look at tabloids and broadsheet newspapers, both during the week and at the weekend.

exam watch

Evaluate critically the way in which a newspaper has handled an issue. Make sure you use appropriate evaluative language and offer clear reasons why you think it could have been handled more effectively.

Examination type questions

a   Describe the variety of religious programmes broadcast on the terrestrial television channels.
(4 marks)

Student's answer

A basic answer to part (a) might be:

Television companies are required by law to broadcast religious programmes, although not much time is given to them compared to, say, sport. There is, however, a variety of religious programmes on all channels …
(1 mark)

To get more marks, your answer needs to be more specific, like this:

… The programmes fall into three main types — worship, magazine-type shows and documentaries. They are usually shown on Sunday mornings or evenings … (2 marks)

To get full marks, you need to write more and evaluate the programmes, like this:

… Songs of Praise is a Christian worship programme, usually showing church services or other types of worship. It also provides the words to religious songs, presumably so that people watching at home can participate in the worship too. The Heaven and Earth Show is a magazine programme which goes out on Sunday mornings. It includes features and discussions on a wide range of religious and moral issues. Religious documentaries tend to be infrequent and often go out late on Sunday evenings. They deal with controversial issues such as abortion, homosexuality and women priests. One such programme is called Witness. (4 marks)

This is now a full answer, with good examples and a clear explanation of the variety of religious programmes. An excellent answer might read like this:

Religious broadcasting is a legal requirement and although the television channels do not offer as much religious broadcasting as they do other areas, such as sport or entertainment, there is a surprisingly wide range of religious programmes available on terrestrial channels. Specifically religious programmes are essentially divided into two categories: worship and magazine programmes, and religious documentaries. To be specifically religious, the programme must be aimed at least at a 'vaguely religious' audience and the religious theme must be dominant throughout.

Worship and magazine programmes include Songs of Praise and The Heaven and Earth Show. Songs of Praise is a weekly programme broadcast early on Sunday evenings, which not only includes worship songs and hymns from different congregations each week, but also magazine items focusing on Christians in the area, church projects and solo musical items. The heart of the programme is Christian music, but it includes topics of human interest. The Heaven and Earth Show is also a magazine programme, shown on Sunday mornings, which covers a wide range of issues of belief in the modern day. It includes articles about issues relevant to all the major faiths, and to New Age spirituality. It is presented in a contemporary format, and encourages audience participation in the studio and from viewers at home.

Religious documentaries appear on all the main channels and cover everything from the lives of prominent modern-day Christians to dramatic reconstructions of the lives of biblical characters. For example, a recent series aimed to reconstruct the life and role of Mary, examining common rumours such as she was raped by a Roman soldier. Another programme followed the life of Moses and examined the ten plagues, offering natural explanations for them all. Running for God looked at the lives of three Christian women who were preparing to run in the Commonwealth Games, and investigated the role their faith played in their approach to sport. These were one-off programmes, but some run more regularly. Witness on Channel 4, for example, is screened at regular intervals and deals with controversial issues within religion, aiming to cover 'a range of stories that collide with faith, identity and belief'. (4 marks)

b Explain the way in which a religious or moral issue has been tackled in a film or television drama. (8 marks)

Student's answer

A basic answer to part (b) might be:

The television drama that I have examined is Priest, made in 1994 and starring Linus Roache and Robert Carlyle. It is the controversial story of a young Roman Catholic Priest who goes to work in a tough inner city Catholic parish in Liverpool. He works with an older priest who preaches a very liberal message, and a bishop who is deeply conservative and traditional in outlook. The story deals with a range of issues, but the central focus is on the fact that the young priest is a secret homosexual, something that is forbidden in the Catholic priesthood … (2 marks)

To get more marks, your answer needs more detail, like this:

… The priest falls in love with another man, but tries to keep it a secret and even denies it before the man. He is arrested for indecency, but soon released. However, as the priest wrestles with his conscience and his shame, he attempts suicide. He recovers, only to be rejected by his bishop.

The young priest was a good one, he was well-liked and carried out his duties properly, but he found it difficult to cope with the pressure of his position and the strict position of the Church … (4 marks)

To get full marks, your answer needs to contain a comprehensive explanation and the use of religious terms, like this:

… The priest loves God, but finds it difficult to understand how a God of love can be so apparently cruel. He struggles deeply with his faith and wonders why he, a priest who has lived such a holy life, could be a homosexual. He returns to his Church and, although many of the parishioners reject him, a few accept him for who he is. The film ends with these believers sharing Mass with him.

Priest deals with the really serious issues facing Catholic Priests today. They may not marry and are forbidden to be active homosexuals. This is in line with certain teachings in the Bible, but this position seems to deny these priests the chance of human love in their personal lives. Such a life might lead to great unhappiness and, in our story, could lead to suicide, depression and remorse. The film is a serious challenge to the traditional views of the Roman Catholic Church. (8 marks)

In this final answer, the candidate has offered a full understanding of the issues and given a clear and comprehensive explanation, together with the use of technical terms.

An excellent answer might read like this:

In class we watched the 1997 film Gattaca, which was directed by Andrew Niccol and starred Ethan Hawke and Jude Law. Although the film is essentially a science fiction drama, the director deliberately set out to tackle the issues raised by the spectre of genetic technology, which is becoming increasingly prominent in modern scientific research. Religious believers are concerned about the potential of genetic engineering, which may, one day, enable human beings to design and create babies to specification. We know that the Human Genome Project has revealed many important things about DNA and genetic patterns. In principle, scientists can tell at a very early stage whether a person is likely to suffer from potentially fatal illnesses, have a disposition to alcoholism, violence, or even homosexuality, or whether they will have poor eyesight, a weak heart or a depressive personality.

In *Gattaca*, the director and writer has imagined a society in the 'not too distant future' where this has become a reality. The main character, Vincent, is a child conceived naturally, without the aid of medical technology, in a world where such children are considered to be invalids, 'the new underclass'. His brother, Anton, is conceived using the latest genetic techniques and is healthy, fit, good looking and destined for success, while Vincent is told that his dreams of going into the space programme at Gattaca are doomed to failure. However, he is determined not to be hampered by his poor genetic inheritance and on the black market he buys the genetic identity of a man, Jerome Morrow, a former swimming star with 'an IQ off the register ... the heart of an ox. You could go anywhere with this guy's helix tucked under your arm.' However, although genetically perfect, fate had intervened and he is wheelchair-bound following a car accident.

The film examines the social and ethical problems raised by determining a person's fate by their DNA, not only for Vincent, the invalid, whose 'resume is in his cells', but also Jerome, who was engineered for perfection but found the burden impossible to bear. We learn that Jerome had attempted suicide, unable to cope with having gained only a silver medal as a swimmer. He had not been able to live up to the expectations imposed on him by his genetic perfection. It is not until he gives Vincent his identity that he seems to feel he has been able to do anything of value.

The film asks 'What happens when man interferes with God's work?' and in the opening credits a quotation from Ecclesiastes flashes up on the screen: 'Consider God's handiwork. Who can straighten what he has made crooked?' The consequences are subtle, not least that society makes judgements about people that limit their potential and frustrate their ability to be their true selves – both Vincent and Jerome were victims of such limiting and controlling assumptions. Neither feels truly free, but determined by their genetic package, which are not even those God had designed, but man.

(8 marks)

Examiner's comment for answer (b)

The strength of this answer lies in the way the candidate has resisted a re-telling of the story and made sure that they have concentrated on the issues raised by the film. Enough narrative is there for us to understand how the issues have been dealt with – the dramatic framework that enables the film to address them – but the answer focuses on using the narrative details to discuss the issues. The candidate knows the film well enough to use direct quotations from the dialogue, which make the answer truly authentic. This is the kind of familiarity you need with the film you choose to watch and analyse in order to make your answer really stand out.

c 'Television programmes never show religious believers as having any serious contribution to make to society.' Do you agree? Give reasons for your opinion, showing you have considered another point of view. Your answer should refer to specific television programmes. (8 marks)

Student's answer

I do not agree with this statement, as there is far more religious broadcasting than we might originally think, and most of it deals with religious people in a fair and unbiased way. However, the minority of programmes fail to do so and it is easy to see why they may lead people to this opinion.

Most religious broadcasting deals with religious people's faith as having significance not only to them, but to society as a whole. Programmes that examine sophisticated religious and philosophical themes, such as Soul Searching, which examined questions about the soul – whether it exists, whether God placed it there – do not trivialize religion but expose important issues that are not just of concern to religious believers, but to all humans. Religious documentaries usually take an academic position on the subjects they are discussing, and although they may not come up with a conclusion that all religious people would agree with (that would be virtually impossible, anyway), they present their evidence in a fair way. Such documentaries recognise that for religious believers there are important implications for them in, for example, attempting to prove the resurrection, or, as Everyman does, examining moral and religious issues, such as inter-faith marriages or euthanasia.

However, there are some programmes that are quite biased in their approach. We watched a video of a documentary shown on Channel 4 in 2000, called Miracles. This followed the work of the international evangelist Benny Hinn, who is the focus of huge rallies or crusades where people come expecting to be healed from cancer, arthritis, paralysis or brain damage. Although the programme showed some people who were genuinely committed to Hinn's work and were expecting a miracle to happen, the programme adopted a very sceptical position and effectively accused Hinn of being a fraud and practising hypnosis on the crowds that came to his crusades. Interestingly, they used religious figures as well as psychologists to criticize Hinn, which may have given an illusion of fairness, but it seemed that they had already made up their minds and were not really examining all the evidence. In this case, it was clear that the programme did not intend the viewer to think that religious people had anything valuable to offer society.

Another problem in the presentation of religious people is the way they sometimes are depicted in dramas and soaps. Soap operas such as EastEnders rarely include a character who is a genuine religious believer, but rather people who are nominally religious, or even a caricature of a believer, such as Dot Cotton. She is presented as being judgemental and intolerant, quoting Bible verses out of context, and when she had a crisis of faith after being mugged, the programme did not show her belonging to a community of fellow believers who could support her, but as being rather isolated. This does not reflect the life and attitudes of most modern Christians, and can lead to a very negative view of the contribution they can make to society. Since many people only ever encounter a Christian on television rather than in their own lives, it is important that Christians are presented as being genuine people, not stereotypes.

(8 marks)

Checklist for revision

	Understand and know	Need more revision	Do not understand
The relationship between the media and religion	☐	☐	☐
Range of religious programmes	☐	☐	☐
Religious and moral themes in soaps	☐	☐	☐
Religious and moral themes in film	☐	☐	☐
Religious and moral themes in newspapers	☐	☐	☐

exam watch

You should base your answers to questions in this section on Christianity and one other religion.

What do I need to know?

- The teachings of Christianity and one other religion on possession; uses and dangers of wealth; **stewardship**, **almsgiving** and charity; compassion and justice; and the relationship between rich and poor.

- The need for world development in response to the causes, extent and effects of poverty in the world.

- The work of religious agencies in world development and the relief of poverty.

- Detailed knowledge of one religious agency and the reasons for its work.

- The relationship of religion to wealth and poverty.

- Knowledge of the work of one individual and their contribution to the relief of poverty.

Wealth and poverty

The wealth of the world is not divided equally. There are some nations and individuals who have great wealth and there are those who have very little and live in a state of hardship and poverty. Most religious believers feel that it is vitally important for the wealth of the world to be more fairly distributed, so that suffering may be relieved and so that all people may have a decent standard of living.

Wealth generally means money, land, **possessions** and often the power, influence and authority that comes with wealth. In the UK people may be particularly wealthy for a number of reasons:

- they have highly paid jobs

- they have inherited wealth

- they have made speculative investments that have paid off

- they are successful in business.

Poverty is a lack of wealth and, therefore, of power. There are different kinds of poverty. The most obvious is the absence of money and material possessions, but poverty can also be of the spirit, where people lack self-respect and love. The main causes of poverty in the UK are:

- unemployment

- homelessness

- poor education and limited opportunities

- alcohol, drugs, gambling or a combination of addictions

- poor mental or physical health, which may lead to any of these other related causes of poverty.

To some extent, what makes a person wealthy or poor depends on where they live. In the Western world, a person might be thought to be rich if they have lots of

key idea

'You cannot serve both God and Money.'
(Matthew 6: 24)

money, whereas someone may be considered poor simply if they earn less. This is called **relative poverty**. By contrast, **absolute poverty** describes those living in a poor country who literally have nothing. In a nation where there is absolute poverty, it would be considered ridiculous to think that somebody could be considered poor if they were living on less than £200 a week. Yet in the UK, this may well be thought, by some, to be the case.

The Christian viewpoint

In the modern world, religious believers tend to see poverty as something that should be fought against. However, this was not always the case, and until relatively recently the Church taught that poverty and wealth were to be accepted as God's will and a matter outside human control (rather like whether you are tall or short). One of the best-loved hymns of the nineteenth century, 'All things bright and beautiful', expressed this view and, as a result, the offending verse is now not usually found in hymnbooks!

The rich man in his castle
The poor man at his gate
God made them high and lowly
And ordered their estate.

The Bible teaches that the poor are very special to God and that, in some cases, wealth separates a person from God, while those who are poor may be able to draw closer to him.

'*Blessed are the poor in spirit, for theirs is the kingdom of Heaven.*' (Matthew 5: 3)

This is not because wealth itself is a bad thing. What is important is how wealth is used. Like most things, it can be used for good or bad purposes. Being wealthy is not against Christian teaching, but greed for possessions is.

'*Do not store up for yourselves treasures on earth, where moth and rust destroy, and where thieves break in and steal. But store up for yourselves treasures in Heaven.*' (Matthew 6: 19–20)

'*For the love of money is a root to all kinds of evil.*' (1 Timothy 6: 10)

Some Christians might think that wealth can be a dangerous thing if used wrongly. For instance, it is easy for rich people to feel they have everything but fail to acknowledge and worship God. Instead they seek more money and material possessions, and money becomes their god insofar as it becomes the thing they trust and rely on.

Christians believe that wealth is a gift from God and should be used for the good of everyone. This means that people who have wealth are 'stewards'. Stewardship means taking care of something (such as wealth) that does not belong to you and using it responsibly. It is often used to describe the relationship that humankind is supposed to have with the natural world, but can be applied to anything for which we are given responsibility.

Jesus advised those who care too much for themselves and their possessions to sell what they have and give their money to the poor.

'*Go, sell everything you have and give to the poor, and you will have treasure in Heaven.*' (Mark 10: 21)

read more

Have a look at a GCSE sociology book. You will find some very interesting information about poverty in the UK.

key idea

The key words in the quotations from Matthew and 1 Timothy opposite are '*store up*' and '*love*'. The second, however, is often quoted wrongly and people think it reads 'money is the root of all evil'. That is not

beware

You cannot be credited if you say that Jesus or God, or any of the biblical writers, taught that it was sinful to be wealthy.

He taught that, *'It is easier for a camel to go through the eye of a needle than for a rich man to enter the kingdom of God.'* (Mark 10: 25)

Christians generally think that wealth should be used to do good and that they have a moral responsibility to use their wealth to help the poor. Some think that God will judge them according to how much concern they have had for the poor.

'If anyone has material possessions and sees his brother in need but has no pity on him, how can the love of God be in him?' (1 John 3: 17)

'"Lord, when did we see you hungry and feed you, or thirsty and give you something to drink?" … "I tell you the truth, whatever you did for one of the least of these brothers of mine, you did for me."' (Matthew 25: 37, 40)

Christians should only obtain wealth in a lawful and moral way – not, for example, through methods that involve harm or exploitation of others, such as crime, pornography or drugs. It is important for people to have the qualities of compassion and justice to offer to others – and greed and exploitation can ruin these qualities.

key idea

'True happiness is not found in riches.' (Catechism of the Catholic Church)

Christian charity

Poverty causes human suffering and is, therefore, a serious concern for Christians. Churches today emphasize the need for the wealthy to share what they have with the poor because caring for the poor is one of the most important ways in which believers can show their love for God. This is the principle of agape (unconditional love) – loving others without expecting anything back in return. The expression of agape is a reflection of the equality of all human beings in the eyes of God, and the truth that his provision on earth is for all humanity and not just for the wealthy.

'Rich nations should have a responsibility to those who cannot develop themselves.' (Catechism of the Catholic Church)

key idea

'The Church should concern itself … with the poor and needy.' (Catechism of the Catholic Church)

Moreover, the Bible teaches that wealthy Christians should set aside some of their money and give it to the poor. This is called almsgiving or charity and is an important part of a Christian's life.

'On the first day of every week, each one of you should set aside a sum of money in keeping with his income.' (1 Corinthians 16: 2)

Some Christians do this by committing to a **tithe**. This is when they set aside 10 per cent of their gross income (*before*, not *after* tax) to give to their church. They may also give further 'offerings' on top of this in response to particular needs that may arise in their community or in the world. Some churches demand this of their members; others leave it to individuals to make a choice whether to tithe. Some consider 10 per cent of net (after tax earnings) to be sufficient; others insist that it should be 10 per cent of gross earnings. Most Christians who tithe believe that God will bless their finances so that they never feel the loss of the tithe.

Some Christians, however, believe that tithing is an Old Testament principle which was overthrown by Jesus, who was critical of Pharisaic tithing practices.

''Woe to you, teachers of the law and Pharisees, you hypocrites! You give a tenth of your spices - mint, dill and cummin. But you have neglected the more important matters of law, justice, mercy and faithfulness. (Matthew 23: 23)

The teachings of Islam

Muslims believe that everything in the world belongs to God, including the material possessions of humans. Wealth and possessions are given as a gift, on loan, by God, and Muslims should, at any time, be prepared to return them to him. Since no one other than God has a choice of who is born rich or poor, all Muslims have a duty to provide for those who are in need. Islam teaches that there is no sense in hoarding material possessions or having a greedy attitude towards wealth when a person's eternal destiny could be at stake.

'And spend of your substance in the cause of Allah, and make not your own hands contribute to your destruction; but do good; for Allah loveth those who do good.' (Surah 2: 195)

Islamic teaching on wealth and poverty is exemplified by the practice of zakah – that is, giving 2.5 per cent of savings and income to the relief of poverty among the Muslim community. This is also an act of devotion as well as charity, since giving zakah purifies a person's money and protects them. The principle of Sadaqah also encourages Muslims to give further, voluntary sums of money when approached or if they have money over and above what they need for the support of their families. This is quite different zakah. Zakah is administered through the mosque, which will deal with applications for financial aid from mosques overseas. The Qur'an specified those groups of people who would most benefit from zakah:

- the poor and needy
- those who are employed to administer zakah
- new converts
- slaves
- debtors

read more

Read the parable of the sheep and goats (Matthew 25: 31–46); the story of the rich young man (Mark 10: 17–31); the widow's offering (Mark 12: 41–4); the parable of the Good Samaritan (Luke 10: 25–37); and the parable of the rich fool (Luke 12: 13–21); and the parable of the rich man and Lazarus (Luke 16: 19–31).

key idea

'He is not a believer who eats his fill while his neighbour remains hungry by his side.' (Hadith Muslim)

- those who work for Islam

- the homeless and strangers ('wayfarers').

Most people will give zakah anonymously, since the Qur'an discouraged making a public show of generosity. No one checks up on payment of zakah either, and it is up to the conscience of each individual whether or not they pay it. Being willing to pay zakah is a test of how prepared a Muslim is to let go of their possessions and to use it to increase justice and goodness in the world.

Islam is strictly opposed to charging interest on loans, since the practice of giving loans serves to impose further financial burdens on the borrower. Hence, Muslims are encouraged to help the poor by giving interest-free loans or to give them money as a gift.

key idea

'By no means shall ye attain righteousness unless ye give freely of that which ye love and whatever ye give, of a truth Allah knoweth it well.'
(Surah 3:92)

Relief of poverty in the UK

In the UK, one of the big questions relates to who is responsible for the relief of poverty. Does the government have an obligation to help those who are in situations of poverty? Or should it be left to local communities and charities?

The Salvation Army

In the UK, there are several religious organizations that help in the relief of poverty. One of the best known is the Salvation Army, which was founded by William Booth in 1865 to help the poor in inner cities. It began with Booth and his followers preaching about Christ in streets, pubs and music halls. They appealed to the common people and showed the love of Jesus in very practical ways – by providing soup kitchens to feed the hungry, and running hostels and shelters for the homeless and for single mothers.

Today, the work of the Salvation Army still continues. It provides hostels for the homeless, food for those who sleep rough on the streets and helps to locate people who have gone missing. It also provides rehabilitation centres for alcoholics and drug addicts, and campaigns against drugs and other forms of addiction. In Salvation Army churches (called citadels) there are clubs for young people and families and for the very old. The Salvation Army raises money for its work through collections, by fund-raising at Christmas and through sales of its magazine, called *The War Cry*. It also receives grants from the government and the local authority.

The relief of worldwide poverty

'Rich nations have a grave moral responsibility towards those which are unable to ensure the means of development by themselves.' (Catechism of the Catholic Church)

The Brandt Report of 1980 highlighted the great imbalance between the nations of the world. This report categorized countries according to their wealth status.

- 'Developed countries' are wealthy countries such as the USA, Japan, Australia and those in Western Europe.

- 'Developing countries' are those that are becoming richer, such as Brazil, Mexico and Malaysia.

- 'Less developed countries' are all extremely poor. They include many countries throughout Africa.

The report stated that developed countries, although containing only 25 per cent of the world's population, nevertheless owned about 80 per cent of the world's wealth. Little has changed since 1980.

There are many reasons why some countries in the world are so poor. The most common factors are as follows.

- Debt – most poor countries have to borrow money from rich countries. These debts are expensive and the countries find it difficult to pay them back. With so much of the country's money being used to pay back debts, there is little left to invest in the nation's development.

- Cash crops – many poor countries have to grow 'cash crops' such as cotton, tea and tobacco, which they can sell quickly to make money. This can be a problem if the value of the crop goes down on world markets. Cash crops are grown on land that could be used to grow food, thus agrivating the problem of starvation.

- Natural disasters – a number of poor countries suffer greatly from floods, droughts and earthquakes.

- Wars – a number of poor countries, particularly in Africa, are continually engaged in local wars that destroy crops and homes, and leave thousands without food and a place to live.

Poverty in a war torn country

- Corrupt leaders – in a number of poor countries, the leadership is corrupt and does not distribute resources properly or fairly.

- Population growth – in the poorest countries, the population grows quickly and there are often too many people to feed and provide for. Life expectancy is low and many die young.

There are many different aid agencies that seek to relieve poverty throughout the world. Some are affiliated to religions while others, such as Oxfam, Comic Relief and Live Aid, have no religious background at all.

Many Christians believe that it is not possible to love God if they ignore the needs of other human beings. Christianity teaches that every human being is valuable to God and that all life is precious and sacred (the principle of the sanctity of life). Remembering that Jesus himself cared for the poor, many Christian aid agencies have been established to follow Christ's example, and relieve poverty throughout the world.

Christian Aid

'*We commit ourselves to strive for a new earth transformed by an end to poverty to promote the dignity and basic rights of every person.*' (Christian Aid vision and values)

key idea
If a country is poor, then it can enter a cycle of suffering. A lack of money means that there may be no schools or clean water, leading to a lack of education and disease, and so no one is able to escape poverty.

beware
However much you know about a non-religious relief organization, you will get no marks at all if you write about them when you have been asked to write about a religious organization.

Christian Aid is an organization that was set up by the British Council of Churches after the Second World War to help refugees made homeless after the war and to help to relieve poverty around the world. Its aim is to help people to help themselves, so that they do not need aid in the future.

'*We will work with those who are committed to supporting poor and marginalized communities to eradicate poverty and promote basic rights and justice.*' (Christian Aid statement of intent)

As a Christian organization, it works through groups of Christians who live in the country concerned and who best know the local problems and how to deal with them. It raises money through donations, fund-raising and collections. Each May since 1957 there has been a Christian Aid week in the UK, with every household receiving an envelope containing information and a request for a donation. This event raises about £10 million every year.

Christian Aid at work in the developing world

About 15 per cent of this money is allocated to emergency aid, a disaster fund that is used to provide immediate help when floods, earthquakes and wars occur. The fund pays for food, medicines, blankets and shelter for the victims. The majority of the rest of the money is used on long-term aid, enabling people to help themselves out of poverty through 'appropriate technology'.

- In Colombia, farmers were shown how to use environmentally friendly farming methods, which saved their homes and lands from developers.

- In Lesotho, Christian Aid financed a local agricultural school to teach farmers more efficient methods of producing food.

- In Afghanistan, and working under dangerous conditions, Christian Aid workers have brought relief to those people made homeless by war.

- In the Middle East, Christian Aid has worked to provide relief for Palestinians in the West Bank and Gaza Strip.

In the UK, Christian Aid tries to educate people so that they realize why there is such a vital need to raise money to help the poorer nations. The Christian Aid news magazine and other educational materials are sent to schools, and the organization campaigns in a number of ways to raise public awareness of the poverty of the world. In recent times, Christian Aid has appointed famous footballers and other celebrities to become their ambassadors in poorer countries, helping to raise the profile of the problems that poverty brings.

✔ **action point**
You can find out more about Christian Aid by sending for its publicity brochures or visiting www.heinemann .co.uk/hotlinks and clicking on this section.

Christian Aid believes in the principle, 'Give a man a fish: feed him for a day. Teach a man to fish: feed him for a lifetime.' What this means is that giving aid without education is ultimately of little value, since it does not equip nations with the skills and resources to break out of the cycle of poverty and become self-reliant.

Christian Aid seeks to change the views and policies of the governments of the rich countries by campaigning for an end to the oppressive debts held by the poorer nations and by encouraging nations to buy the produce of poorer nations at a fair price. Campaigners have challenged the rich nations to offer fairer deals to the poor and to safeguard the weakest and most vulnerable. In November 2001, members of Christian Aid formed part of the Trade Justice Movement that held a large protest in London. In July 2001, campaigners protested outside the G8 summit of the leaders of the wealthiest nations during their meeting in Genoa.

The ethos of Christian Aid is best expressed by the organization itself, in its 'Prayer for a new Earth'.

'God of all places and this place:
you promised a new earth where the hungry will feast
and the oppressed go free.
Come Lord, build that place among us.'

CAFOD

'CAFOD's mission is to promote human development and social justice in witness to Christian faith and Gospel values.' (CAFOD mission statement)

> **key idea**
>
> 'CAFOD looks forward to a world in which … the voice of the poor is heard and heeded by all, and lives are no longer dominated by greed.' (CAFOD vision)

CAFOD, or The Catholic Fund for Overseas Development, was founded in 1962 by the Catholic Bishops of England and Wales. The aim was to provide a focus for all the smaller charitable efforts that were going on at that time and to raise money. It raised £25,000 in the first year, and grew rapidly. Within ten years, it was helping 245 projects worldwide. Today it is involved in the relief of world poverty through more than 1000 programmes worldwide.

The major share of CAFOD's funding comes from the Catholic Community. In 2002–03 Catholic churches, groups and individuals raised almost £20 million for CAFOD's work, together with more than £10 million coming from governments and other donors and agencies. CAFOD works in five main areas.

- Long-term development – helping the world's poorest communities to develop agriculture, education and heath care.

- Emergencies – providing immediate help for people affected by wars, natural disasters and other emergencies.

- Campaigning – on behalf of the world's poor.

- Analysis – of the causes of underdevelopment.

- Education – raising awareness in richer nations of the problems of world poverty.

In recent years, CAFOD has been involved in issues such as campaigning for a total ban against landmines, earthquake relief in El Salvador, and humanitarian aid in Serbia, Latin America and Africa. CAFOD has also actively campaigned to cancel the debt of less developed countries, and CAFOD supporters campaigned outside the G8 summits in Birmingham and Genoa.

Muslim Aid

Muslim Aid, which was founded in 1985, uses donations and legacies to help save and improve the lives of millions of people in 50 of the poorest countries around the world. It responds quickly to emergencies, providing relief to victims of natural disasters, wars and famine. It also responds through more long-term development programmes such as provision of clean water, shelter, education, income generation and healthcare. In this way, like Christian Aid, Muslim Aid aims to tackle the root causes of poverty. Experienced in the field of international relief and development work, Muslim Aid focuses on working in partnership with local community-based organizations that help to build the capacity of local people to help themselves, re-gain their dignity and feel less helpless. Muslim Aid also runs offices in crisis areas which directly provide relief and development projects – including three field offices in Sudan, Bangladesh and Somalia, which employ over 60 local staff.

Muslim Aid providing relief

Since its foundation, Muslim Aid has helped people affected by war, famine, flooding, earthquakes and other natural disasters, in Palestine, Afghanistan, Bangladesh, Jamaica, Ethiopia, Angola, Bosnia, Chechnya, Kosova, Cambodia and many others.

Christian missionaries: Mother Teresa Of Calcutta (1910–1997)

Mother Teresa was born Agnes Bojaxhiu, in Skopje, Macedonia in 1910 and became one of the most famous Christian missionaries and aid workers of the twentieth century. She was raised in a poor but devoted Christian family. Despite being poor, her mother always shared food with other poor people, whom, she told her young daughter, were 'God's special people'. This stayed with young Agnes all her life. At the age of seventeen, she became a nun and took a religious name, Teresa. Soon after, she was sent to India to teach poor children and stayed there for seventeen years, eventually becoming headmistress of her school.

Teresa was devoted to looking after the poor and destitute. On 10 September 1946, which became known as Inspiration Day by those she worked with, Teresa believed that God told her to leave her convent to go and live among the poor people she helped. She undertook medical training and moved to Calcutta. With the help of some of her old school pupils, she set up a Christian community of volunteers who would help the needy wherever they found them. Teresa herself wore a blue and white sari, just as the Indian women did.

In 1952, Teresa opened the Nirmal Hriday Home for the Dying (The Place of the Pure Heart). Soon after, despite local opposition, she opened a larger home called the Mother House and her community became known as the Missionaries of Charity. A further home for abandoned children was opened, and a village was built to house lepers and enable them to receive medication until they were cured.

Over the years, Mother Teresa became a figurehead for her work with the poor. She was honoured by the Indian government, by the Pope and by the Queen. In 1979 she received the Nobel Peace Prize. Mother Teresa inspired large numbers of people and touched the consciences of world leaders. Upon receiving the Nobel Prize, she said: '*I am grateful to receive the Prize in the name of the hungry, the naked, the homeless, of the crippled, of the blind, of the lepers, of all those people who feel unloved …*' Today, the Missionaries of Charity have centres in 80 countries and have helped thousands of people. Mother Teresa died on 5 September 1997.

Muslim missionaries

Unlike Christianity, which has a long tradition of missionary work, Islam does not have missionaries as such. Z. Kasmani from Muslim Aid explains why: '*Each individual Muslim is obliged to convey the message of Islam as a monotheistic religion, without coercion, in the best manner - with wisdom, tact and kindness. Often this method is the practical demonstration of living the Islamic way through their own example of good manners, kindness, honesty, compassion for fellow humans, rather than preaching about the religion.*'

Shahid Athar, a Muslim academic, observes that following in the example of Muhammad, every Muslim has an obligation to convey the message of Islam. This is the Muslim missionary task. Athar identifies four tools for the task.

- The missionary should have the highest moral and religious character.

- They should truly believe in what they are preaching.

- They should have an in-depth knowledge of Islam drawn essentially from the Qur'an and the Sunnah (the life of the Prophet), and a knowledge of other major religious traditions in order to make an informed comparison.

- They should be persistent in their work and never lose hope.

Interestingly, Athar identifies a key problem for Muslim missionaries, and that is the successful humanitarian work that Christian missionaries do in Muslim countries. He writes:

'*While we have a better product, they cater better to the humanitarian needs of the poor and destitute in Muslim countries, which should have been our priority to begin with. Christian missionaries are spending thousands and millions of dollars in Muslim countries in relief work, in establishing schools, colleges and hospitals. Are rich Muslim countries and individuals doing the same in non-Muslim countries? Most of the leaders of Muslim countries were educated in a missionary or western school. Thus, taking care of the poor, the sick, the widow and orphan is, and should be, part of Islamic missionary work to non-Muslims.*'

Whilst Islam is not associated with famous missionary figures such as Christianity's Mother Teresa or David Livingstone, along with the obligation placed on all Muslims to convey the teaching and truth of Islam, there are organizations which have a missionary purpose. One such organization is The Qur'an Account, which works in the USA to minister to prison inmates who have converted to Islam whilst serving their sentence. The organization provides new converts with educational tools, and fights on their behalf for the right to be served halal food, and to observe fast and prayer times. The charity's goal is to support new Muslims during their sentence and offer financial and social support upon release. Athar writes: '*If we do not absorb them into society, most likely they will go back to crime, prison and to disbelief.*'

Farida Ahmed Siddiqui, a member of the National Commission on the Status of Women, an organization within the Pakistani government, has established several

> **key idea**
>
> '*One day, a poor person from the street was being washed by Mother Teresa. A visitor came in and said to her, "I would not do that for a million dollars." "Neither do we," Mother Teresa replied. "We do it for love. We do it for Jesus."*'

Islamic missionary schools and the Islamic Missionary University for Women, as well as several centres and Madrassah throughout Karachi. She has also worked with women prisoners in Karachi jail and helped 100 women every year to obtain jehez (bridal gifts).

Sample questions

The extended writing questions have a different structure to the other examination questions, and you have more time in which to do them. However, as with the ordinary examination questions, the more useful and relevant knowledge and evaluation that you put in, the more marks you will get.

The question, like all the others, is marked by levels. The fewest marks are given at Level 1, for simple ideas and examples. Level 2 answers gain higher marks because they contain discussion points and show some understanding of the issues involved. At Level 3, answers gain higher marks because they are well structured and contain more in-depth knowledge and evaluation. The highest marks are awarded at Level 4, where the answer is comprehensive and displays a full understanding of the topic using specialist religious language.

Examination type questions

a Outline the teaching of one religion concerning the relief of poverty. (4 marks)

Student's answer

Christianity teaches that wealth is a gift from God and should be used for the good of everyone. In particular, this means helping the poor. The poor are very special to God: 'Blessed are the poor in spirit, for theirs is the kingdom of Heaven' (Matthew 5: 3). Jesus taught that those who care too much for their possessions should sell what they have and give their money to the poor and told the rich young man who asked him how to enter the kingdom of God that he should: 'Go, sell everything you have and give to the poor, and you will have treasure in Heaven' (Mark 10: 21).

Christian Churches today highlight the need for the wealthy to share what they have with the poor. Caring for the poor is one of the most important ways in which believers can show their love for God. 'The Church should concern itself … with the poor and needy' (Catechism of the Catholic Church). Christians are taught that there are many ways in which they can help the poor. They may choose to live simply themselves, ensuring that they are not wasting their resources or being greedy, and donate regular sums to charities and organizations which help the poor. Many Christians tithe – this is giving 10 per cent of income to the church, which is then responsible for seeing that it is used wisely. It may help the poor within its own local community or make donations on behalf of its members to worldwide relief organizations. Christianity teaches that making public shows of wealth – or of giving – is not in the spirit of Jesus and although they do not teach that wealth is, in itself, wrong, they do teach that to love money and possessions is against God's will, and does not contribute to relief of poverty. (4 marks)

b Explain how the teaching of one religion has enabled an agency to work for the relief of poverty. (8 marks)

Student's answer

CAFOD is a Christian relief agency that works to relieve poverty throughout the world and has more than 1000 programmes worldwide. It provides long-term aid to help the world's poorest communities to develop agriculture, education and heath care. It also provides short-term emergency help for people affected by wars and natural disasters. Part of its work consists of educating the poor and also raising awareness of the issues among people in richer countries, where CAFOD conducts its fund-raising. CAFOD is also involved in a number of campaigns on behalf of the world's poor. Its work is founded on the teachings of the Bible: 'CAFOD's mission is to promote human development and social justice in witness to Christian faith and Gospel values' (CAFOD mission statement).

Following the example of Jesus, members of CAFOD feel that it is important for the wealth of the world to be more fairly distributed, so that suffering may be relieved and so that all people may have a decent standard of living. All people are seen as equal in the eyes of God and God's provision on earth is for all humanity, not just the wealthy: 'If anyone has material possessions and sees his brother in need but has no pity on him, how can the love of God be in him?' (1 John 3: 17)

Underlying the work of CAFOD is the belief that every human being is valuable to God and that all life is precious and sacred. Remembering that Jesus himself cared for the poor, CAFOD seeks to follow Christ's example, and relieve poverty throughout the world. 'CAFOD looks forward to a world in which … the voice of the poor is heard and heeded by all, and lives are no longer dominated by greed' (CAFOD vision).

(8 marks)

Examiner's comments for answers (a) and (b)

These are both good answers. There are clear references to religious teachings, and the candidate has outlined the important issues and produced a coherent description of the teaching, using specialist terms and relevant quotations. The candidate has seen the issue of poverty relief in the context of the overall topic of wealth and poverty, and this has given their answer some real substance.

c   'You cannot be wealthy and religious.' Do you agree? Give reasons for your opinion, showing that you have considered another point of view. In your answer you should refer to at least one religion.

(8 marks)

Student's answer

A basic answer to part (c) might be:

In the Bible, it says that people who are too concerned with money cannot have a proper relationship with God: 'It is easier for a camel to go through the eye of a needle than for a rich man to enter the kingdom of God' (Mark 10: 25). It is not wrong to be wealthy as such, but it is wrong to be greedy …

(1 mark)

To get more marks, your answer needs to be more specific, like this:

… However, if money is used properly, money can be used to do a great deal of good and can help to relieve poverty. The Bible teaches that those with money should help the poor – this is called 'almsgiving'. Indeed, in the Parable of the Good Samaritan, Jesus teaches that a person can use their money for a good purpose and help a suffering person to recover. This is how to use wealth properly and to follow the example of Jesus …

(4 marks)

To get full marks, you must add further information and show greater understanding and evaluation, like this:

… This can be difficult, although wealthy Christians, such as the singer Cliff Richard, do use their money to help others. It is, therefore, possible to be wealthy and religious, since it is not *having money that causes the problem, it is the person's attitude towards money and how they use it. If they are greedy and 'love money' then it will be very hard for them to be truly religious and follow God: 'You cannot serve both God and Money' (Matthew 6: 24).*

The wealthy person, then, must use their money to help others and should avoid spending their time trying to get even more money. In that way they can stay close to God. It is very hard, not least because other people may be jealous of their riches. Indeed, several wealthy religious believers have wondered if it would be better not to admit they are religious at all. (8 marks)

This is a comprehensive answer, using religious language, biblical references and covering the argument from both side – full marks!

An excellent answer to this question might read like this:

The Bible teaches that wealth can make it difficult when it comes to having a relationship with God. People who are too concerned with their wealth cannot find God: 'It is easier for a camel to go through the eye of a needle than for a rich man to enter the kingdom of God' (Mark 10: 25). It is not wrong to be wealthy, but it is wrong to be greedy. The danger of wealth is that people tend to forget about God and seek more and more money. 'You cannot serve both God and Money' (Matthew 6: 24).

However, used properly, wealth can do a great deal of good and can help to relieve poverty. The Bible teaches that wealthy Christians should give some of their money to the poor. This is called almsgiving and is an important part of a Christian's life: 'On the first day of every week, each one of you should set aside a sum of money in keeping with his income' (1 Corinthians 16: 2). In the Parable of the Good Samaritan, Jesus teaches that a good man is able to use his money for good purposes, when he helps a man who is suffering to recover. Through his wealth he is able to help and follow the example of Christ. It is sometimes difficult to see how this might apply to Christians today, however, as there tend to be few wealthy Christians in the public eye who are using their wealth for the benefit of others. The singer and entertainer Cliff Richard is a wealthy Christian who seems to be a good example, however. Apparently, the writer John Grisham is a Christian, and it would be interesting to know if he tithes to his church. If so, they should be very rich!

In conclusion, therefore, it is possible to be wealthy and religious, but it is hard. To achieve it, a wealthy person must understand that their money should be used wisely, to help others, and they should not spend their lives greedily seeking more. In that way, they will be able to stay close to God and keep track of his will for their lives. One of the biggest difficulties they may face, though, is the attitudes of other people who begrudge them their wealth and make them feel that having money leaves them with no option but not to admit to being a Christian. (8 marks)

Checklist for revision

	Understand and know	Need more revision	Do not understand
The teaching of Christianity and one other religion on wealth and poverty	☐	☐	☐
Relief of poverty in the UK	☐	☐	☐
Relief of poverty worldwide	☐	☐	☐
Work of one religious organization for the relief of poverty	☐	☐	☐

Answers to short questions

1 Believing in God

A miracle is an act that breaks a natural law and is thought to be brought about by God. It could be a healing from a terminal illness or a recovery from paralysis. Miracles always have good outcomes. (2 marks)

2 Matters of life and death

The term 'sanctity of life' refers to the notion that God is the creator of human life and that people are made in God's image. Life is, therefore, a sacred gift from God. (2 marks)

3 Marriage and the family

Re-marriage means marrying again after being divorced from a previous marriage. (2 marks)

4 Social harmony

Prejudice is an attitude that judges people before we know them on the basis of their race, religion, gender, sexual orientation, or any other aspect of them that we think singles them out as being different from us. (2 marks)

Glossary

The definitions of the words listed here are given in the strictest, most traditional terms. Bear in mind, however, they may be open to a wider range of interpretations, which you may like to discuss with your teacher. Nevertheless, the definitions given here will always be considered correct when used in an exam.

Abortion The removal of a foetus from the womb before it can survive

Absolute poverty Conditions in which people have no money, land or possessions

Active euthanasia Taking active steps to end the life of a patient – for example, a lethal injection

Adultery An act of sexual intercourse between a married person and someone other than their marriage partner

Agape love Love that does not expect anything in return; used to describe the ideal Christian love as exemplified by Jesus

Agnostic A person who is unsure whether God exists

All-knowing *See Omniscient*

All-loving *See Benevolent*

All-powerful *See Omnipotent*

Almsgiving Charitable donations

Assisted suicide Providing a seriously ill person with the means to commit suicide

Atheist Someone who believes that God does not exist

Benevolent The belief that God is good/kind

Causation The idea that everything has been caused (started off) by something else

Charismatic Experiences inspired by the Holy Spirit, including speaking in tongues and prophecy

Cohabitation Living together without being married

Communion of saints The belief that Christians will live on after death and continue to be part of the Christian community on earth

Contraception Preventing conception from occurring

Conversion When your life is changed by giving yourself to God

Cumulative argument Several arguments for the existence of God put together to create a stronger case

Design argument The principle that things that have a purpose and function and have been designed for that purpose, including the universe

Divorce The legal termination of a marriage

Dualism The view that there are two natures to everything: a physical (seen) and spiritual (unseen)

Empirical evidence Evidence confirmed by use of the senses

Equality The state of everyone having equal rights regardless of gender/race/class

Eternal The belief that God exists without beginning and end

Euthanasia An easy and gentle death

Exclusivism The view that only those who belong to one particular faith can be saved from condemnation

Extended family Children, parents and grandparents/aunts/uncles living as a unit or in close proximity

Heaven A place of paradise where God rules

Hell A place of horrors where Satan rules

Heterosexuality Sexual attraction to members of the opposite sex

Homosexuality Sexual attraction to members of the same sex

Immortal soul A soul that can live on after the death of the physical body

Inclusivism The view that all religions have some truth, and should be able to teach and practise without restriction or prejudice

Inconsistent triad The logical problem of how evil can exist and an omnipotent, all-loving God can also exist

Involuntary euthanasia Ending the life of a patient when they are not able to make the request for themselves

Marriage The condition of a man and woman legally united for the purpose of living together and, usually, having children

Media The media of mass communication, usually including television, radio, newspapers and film

Miracle Something which seems to break a law of science and makes you think only God could have done it

Moral evil Actions done by humans which cause suffering

Multi-ethnic society Many different races and cultures living together in one society

Multi-faith society Many different religions living together in one society

Multi-racial society Many different races living together in one society

Mystical experience Hearing God's voice or seeing a vision of a religious figure

Natural evil Things which cause suffering but have nothing to do with humans – for example, earthquakes

Near-death experience An experience after clinical death when a patient may see bright lights, a religious figure, and sense that they are being being sent back to earth

Non-voluntary euthanasia Ending someone's life painlessly when they are unable to ask, but you have good reason for thinking they would want you to do so – for example, switching off a life-support machine

Nuclear family Mother, father and children living as a unit

Numinous The feeling of the presence of something greater than you – for example, in a church or looking up at the stars

Omnipotent The belief that God is all-powerful

Omniscient The belief that God knows everything that has happened and everything that is going to happen

Paranormal Unexplained things which are thought to have spiritual causes – for example, ghosts and mediums

Passive euthanasia Withdrawing medical treatment or nourishment to hasten the death of a patient

Possessions Things that people possess or own

Poverty Lack of money, land and possessions

Prayer An attempt to contact God, usually through words

Prejudice Believing that some people are inferior or superior without even knowing them

Pre-marital sex Sex before marriage

Promiscuity Having sex with a number of partners without commitment

Purgatory A place where Catholics believe souls go after death to be purified

Racial Relating to matters of race

Racial discrimination Treating people less favourably and considering them to be less worthy on the grounds of their race

Racial harmony Different races/colours living together happily

Racism The belief that some races are superior to others

Reconstituted family Where two sets of children (step-brothers and sisters) become one family when their divorced parents marry each other

Relative poverty Making judgements about poverty in a society where most people have some money, land or possessions

Religious experience An experience that conveys a sense of the presence of God

Religious freedom The right to practice your religion and change your religion

Religious pluralism Accepting all religions as having an equal right to coexist

Re-marriage Marrying again after being divorced from a previous marriage

Resurrection The belief that, after death, the body stays in the grave until the end of the world when it is raised

Sanctity of life The belief that life is holy and belongs to God

Secular A non-religious view, society or organization

Sexism Discriminating against people because of their gender (being male or female)

Single parent family One parent living alone with their children; this may be due to divorce, separation, the death of the other partner or because the parent is unmarried

Stewardship Looking after something so it can be passed onto the next generation

Tithe Committing 10 per cent of your income to the church or other religious organization (Christianity)

Tokenism Including a minority figure simply to ensure that there can be no claim made of racism

Verified When something is proven to be true

Voluntary euthanasia The situation where someone dying in pain asks a doctor to end her/his life painlessly

Wealth Money, land and possessions

Zakah The tax Muslims pay for the poor (2.5 per cent of income)

Index